Scotland's Environment

Scotland's Environment: The Future

Edited by

George Holmes and Roger Crofts

Tuckwell Press in association with
The Royal Society of Edinburgh
and
Scottish Natural Heritage

First published in Great Britain by
Tuckwell Press
The Mill House
Phantassie
East Linton
East Lothian EH40 3DG
Scotland

Copyright © The Editors and Contributors severally, 2000

ISBN 1 86232 162 0

British Library Cataloguing in Publication Data

A catalogue record for this book is available
on request from the British Library

Typeset by Hewer Text Ltd, Edinburgh
Printed and bound by The Cromwell Press, Trowbridge

Contents

PART FOUR. OVERVIEW

List of Contributors

Professor John Bryden, Co-Director of Arkleton Centre for Rural Development Research, University of Aberdeen.

Professor Melvin Cannell, FRSE, Head of Edinburgh Research Station, Institute of Terrestrial Economy, NERC.

Professor Roger Crofts, CBE, Chief Executive, Scottish Natural Heritage.

Professor Kevin Edwards, Department of Geography, University of Aberdeen.

Dr John M Francis, FRSE, UK Commission, UNESCO.

Professor Nick Hanley, Institute of Ecology and Resource Management, University of Edinburgh.

Dr Keith Hart, Arkleton Centre for Rural Development Research, University of Aberdeen.

Ms Patricia Henton, Chief Executive, Scottish Environmental Protection Agency.

Sir Martin Holdgate, CB, Former Director-General of IUCN – The World Conservation Union.

Dr George Holmes, CB, FRSE, Chairman of Organising Committee.

Douglas Macmillan, Department of Agriculture, University of Aberdeen.

Professor Jeff Maxwell, OBE, FRSE, Director, Macaulay Land Use Research Institute, Aberdeen.

Professor Jeremy Peat, Chief Economist, The Royal Bank of Scotland, Edinburgh.

Professor T C Smout, CBE, FRSE FBA, FSA (Scot), Director, Institute for Environmental History, University of St Andrews and Historiographer Royal in Scotland.

Introduction

George Holmes and Roger Crofts

FOR SOME YEARS, the Royal Society of Edinburgh (RSE) and Scottish Natural Heritage (SNH) (see Appendices 4 and 5) have jointly organised an annual lecture. The aim has been to invite a speaker of international renown to discuss fundamental environmental issues and to stimulate discussion and debate amongst the many constituent interests in Scotland with interest in the responsibility for the environment. Previous lectures have covered a wide range of topics within the spirit of global environmental responsibility and the importance of the link between environmental stewardship, social wellbeing and economic prosperity.

The two organisations felt that their joint event for the year 2000 should be of a more seminal nature. The beginning of the new Millennium is an opportune time for both looking back and for looking forward. The establishment of the Scottish Parliament and the Scottish Executive with devolved responsibilities for many environmental and other relevant issues is also an opportune moment to stimulate discussion and debate and, hopefully, stimulate action for Scotland's environment for the future.

The RSE and SNH established an organising committee to plan and execute a one-day Millennium conference, 'The Future for the Environment in Scotland: Resetting the Agenda?'. George Holmes, as convenor and Roger Crofts representing SNH, were helped in their work by Professors John Beck, Geoffrey Boulton, Chris Smout and Roger Wheater, and we thank our colleagues for their help.

In addition, we took the view that any debate on the future of the environment in Scotland must take account of the views of younger generations. With the help of the educational staff of the RSE, we also convened a one-day workshop, 'Scotland's Environment: What Future?' at which students from secondary fourth to sixth years from around Scotland focused on the interplay between tourism and the environment within the broader framework of sustainable development. The outcome of this Forum is presented as Chapter 8 in this volume.

This volume comprises the proceedings of the conference, the structure of which was designed to address five very broad questions relating to the environment and especially the rural environment of Scotland:

1. What are the indications from recent history? Kevin Edwards and Chris Smout review the results of interactions between society and the environment in the past.
2. Where are present trends taking us? Jeff Maxwell and Melvin Cannell offer some views on the likely nature of the environment and land uses in the future.
3. What are the main drivers of change? Jeremy Peat examines the influence of economic factors, and John Francis reflects on ethical issues and changing public values.
4. What should be our future aims? Tricia Henton and Roger Crofts set out some key issues and objectives for sustainable development.
5. What policy instruments will be required to achieve these aims? Nick Hanley and Douglas Macmillan examine economic instruments, and John Bryden and Keith Hart discuss ways of fostering environmental stewardship of land.

Finally, Martin Holdgate summarises the papers and discussion. As a result of the conference we have prepared a short 'Agenda for Action' setting out what we believe to be the main conclusions and recommendations. Its contents do not necessarily reflect the view of the RSE or SNH.

We hope that the chapters which follow, including the 'Agenda for Action' and the stimulating input from teenagers, will help to clarify objectives and attract support for improving Scotland's environment in the future.

We wish to record our thanks to other members of the organising committee, to financial sponsors, especially Scottish Natural Heritage and the Scottish Environmental Protection Agency, and to the staff in the RSE and SNH who have provided support. Particular thanks go to Steve Atkins, Veronica Burbridge and Clive Mitchell of SNH for their help in preparing the 'Agenda for Action', and Linda Nicholls for typing support.

Part One. Setting the Scene

1

Perspectives on Human-Environment Interactions in Prehistoric and Historical Times

K J Edwards and T C Smout

INTRODUCTION

THIS CONTRIBUTION MIGHT be thought to sit uncomfortably amongst a series of papers addressing the future for the rural environment in Scotland, with an interrogative look at a resetting of the agenda. In the first place, our brief is to examine the past and not the future, and secondly, the past for many people was probably one bereft of an agenda other than to live, love and die with a minimum of fuss and hardship! It is difficult, however, to appreciate the present, let alone to divine trajectories for the future, without a consideration of the past, and we shall unashamedly indulge our passions for this while at the same time constantly hinting at its relevance to the deliberations of this conference.

The temporal context for this paper is set by the first expansion of agriculture some 6000 calendar years ago through to the present. Clearly, several conferences could be devoted profitably to the elucidation of such a theme, and we shall be forced to be extremely selective in our exposition. It might be appropriate to begin by stating that evidence for much of the last few millennia is patchy to say the least. Maps of the last few centuries can indicate to varying degrees the distribution of population and its environmental setting. Prior to this we are reliant upon the survival of documents, or more typically the survival and discovery of archaeological monuments. When it comes to the environment and its landscape setting, then much dependence is placed upon proxy evidence for environmental change supplied by the methods of Quaternary science, including pollen analysis, bioarchaeology, pedology, sedimentology and palaeoclimatology.[1] In other words, fossil plant and animal remains and the soils and sediments which contain them can

3

yield their own powerful records of human and environmental history.

But how did people interact with their environment in the past and were their endeavours successful? In many ways this is the story of a changing resource base and the environment is key and integral to happenings over the last few millennia. *We* may be concerned about global warming and the price of sheep, but woodland destruction, soil deterioration and climate change would all have influenced activities in prehistoric and historical times.

BEGINNINGS AND THE ESTABLISHMENT OF PATTERNS

The choice of 6000 years ago is not a random one. The certain expansion of Neolithic agriculture, with arable as well as pastoral farming undertaken by people who were most likely and largely to have been or became sedentary, marks the major economic change in prehistory. The hunter-gatherer lifestyle of Mesolithic peoples was giving way to one which was to have demonstrable and widespread impacts upon the rural environment. The distributions of various types of Neolithic remains may be taken to portray a baseline for prehistoric population distribution (Fig. 1). Attempts have been made to quantify the numbers of people from building size, the skeletal content of tombs, or estimates of the labour requirements for monument construction or for the clearance of woodland. These are little more than heuristic exercises and for the moment, human populations in prehistory, especially at the national level, remain a largely unquantified parameter.[3]

What landscapes confronted the Neolithic agriculturalists, many of whom may have been immigrants to the territory now known as Scotland? Answers are to be found in the studies of palaeoecology – in particular pollen analysis (palynology) which reveals the distribution and nature of past vegetation, and archaeozoology, which, with a less complete data set, is able to outline the past faunal composition. Collectively, they provide an indication of the biodiversity of Scotland since the Neolithic period. An illustration of the appearance of landscapes is given in Figure 2, which indicates that the broad-scale vegetational aspect was one of woodland – even in the Western and Northern Isles which were likely to have had at least a shrubby vegetational cover, dominated by birch (*Betula*) and hazel (*Corylus avellana*) in many areas. The greater part of southern Scotland was covered by mixed woods of oak (*Quercus*), elm (*Ulmus*) and hazel; northern lowlands and coastal areas were characterised by birch, hazel and oakwoods; while the northern uplands had a striking cover of Scots pine (*Pinus sylvestris*) and birch. This vegetational landscape was populated by a vertebrate fauna which included the red deer (*Cervus elephus*), roe deer (*Capreolus capreolus*), elk (*Alces alces*), aurochs (*Bos primigenius*), horse (*Equus ferus*), brown bear (*Ursus arctus*), wolf (*Canis lupus*), boar (*Sus scrofa*) and beaver (*Castor fiber*), as well as a wide range of birds and fish.[4] There was no shortage of fruits, nuts, timber or animal foodstuffs and resources from land and sea. The environment was not entirely natural at this stage – hunter-gatherers had occupied parts of the landscape for at least 5000 years and although not extensive, their impacts would have reduced woodland locally, would have perhaps promoted and maintained heathland by fire in order to attract game[5] and would have led to minor soil erosion.[6]

Added to this less than pristine landscape, were the domesticated biota which became the staple of early farmers in Scotland, *viz.* sheep (*Ovis aries*), cattle (*Bos taurus*), wheat (*Triticum*) and barley (*Hordeum*). Initially their introduction may have been on a small scale, entailing little more than the utilisation of forest openings and modest clearings, but there soon followed the more major clearance of woodland which must surely have constituted an 'artefact' as remarkable as the farming, the settlements and the other monuments within the landscape.

Patterns of woodland reduction, responding to spatially and chronologically discontinuous human activity, may be illustrated by data from two fossil pollen sites (Figs 3 and 4). Black Loch lies in an agriculturally-rich basin in northern Fife.[7] Its woodland was dominated by oak, elm, alder (*Alnus glutinosa*) and hazel. Elm especially was much reduced between about 5200 and 4700 radiocarbon years before present (^{14}C yr BP) (3990 and 3410 calendar [cal] years BC) and as elm often grows on more fertile soils, the reduction may signify selective clearance by axe. Cereal pollen, reflecting arable cultivation, also appears in the fossil record at the site in this interval, though the increase in the pollen of grasses (Poaceae) and pastoral weeds (e.g. *Plantago lanceolata* [ribwort plantain]) demonstrates the importance of pastoral activity. The complexity of this picture is indicated by the fact that the elm decline, a near-synchronous pattern evident across northwest Europe,[8] may have multiple causes including pathogenic attack, climate and soil deterioration, as well as human involvement.

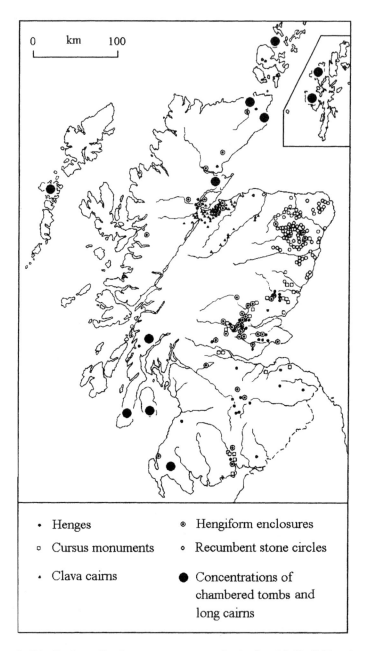

Figure 1: Distributions of various monument types in the Scottish Neolithic, *viz.* henges, hengiform enclosures, cursus monuments, recumbent stone circles, Clava cairns and major concentrations of other chambered tombs and long cairns.[2] Houses, pottery, and isolated artefacts are excluded.

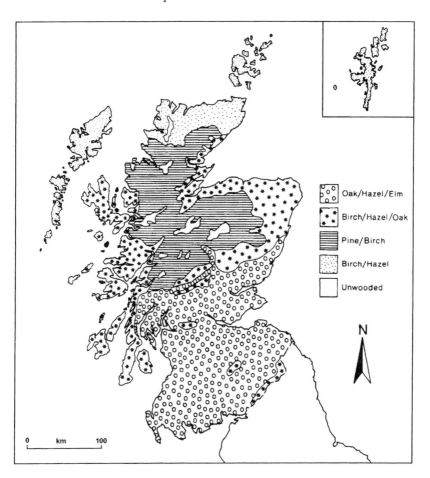

Figure 2: Woodland in Scotland at the time of the early Neolithic (*ca.* 4000 cal BC).

While the patterns at Black Loch apply to much of Scotland, that at Lochan na Cartach, Isle of Barra (Fig. 4) is fairly typical of vegetational behaviour in offshore islands.[9] In contrast to its current unwooded state, birch and hazel, with perhaps local stands of elm, oak, alder and pine, were present until about 6350 ^{14}C yr BP (5270 cal BC). Woodland decline here may have been part of a response to an ongoing climatic process which also involved the spread of blanket peat denoted by the expansions in heather (*Calluna vulgaris*) and sedges (Cyperaceae). The pollen assemblages show signs of probable human impact from a Neolithic date of *ca* 4190 ^{14}C yr BP (2690 cal BC) onwards, when arboreal pollen frequencies fall and herbaceous taxa, including cereal-type, increase their representation. This

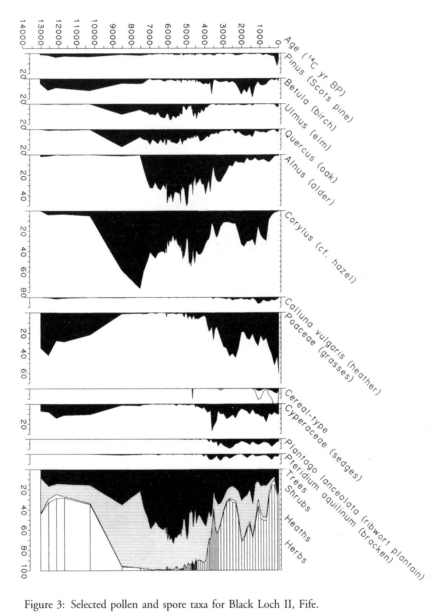

Figure 3: Selected pollen and spore taxa for Black Loch II, Fife.

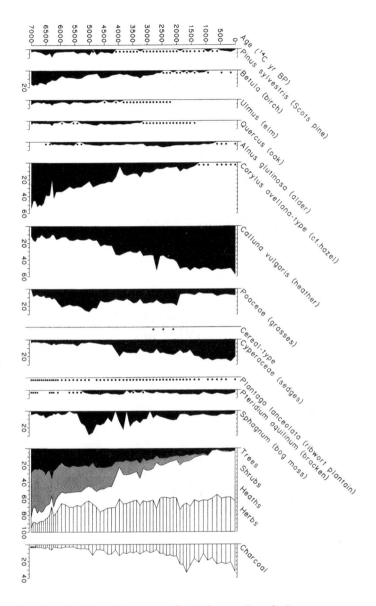

Figure 4: Selected pollen and spore taxa for Lochan na Cartach, Barra.

was, however, also close to the period of the regional *Pinus* decline,[10] when increasing wetness appears to have led to the widespread decline in Scots pine populations. Once again, we are seeing the difficulties of interpretation when multiple causes are probably involved. However, taking account of the distributions of monuments in Figure 2, it is stretching imagination too far to consider that Neolithic and probably larger subsequent human populations did not exert deleterious effects upon their environments.

Before leaving the Neolithic, let us put some archaeological flesh on such an environmental background. On the south bank of the River Dee, in Aberdeenshire, 3 kilometres east of Banchory, lies the remains of the massive Balbridie timber hall measuring 24x12 metres (another broadly similar structure is located on the opposite bank of the river at Crathes). First detected by its crop mark, the excavations at the site produced fragmentary remains of carbonised oak timbers, wheat grains and other plant materials radiocarbon-dated to the period *ca* 3850-3500 cal BC.[11] The plant macrofossil material (bones have barely survived in the acid soils) is notable for its 20,000 cereal grains, the largest assemblage known from the British Isles and comprising emmer wheat (*Triticum dicoccum*), bread wheat (*T. aestivum*) and two kinds of barley including naked barley (*Hordeum vulgare*) – two grains of oats (*Avena*) are assumed to represent weeds in the cereal crop. Cultivated flax (*Linum usitatissimum*) seeds may denote the extraction of oil. The size of the structure indicates that a source of oak timber was required and oak was certainly to be found on Deeside. Pollen contained in turf from a trench (if the turf was local) indicates, however, that stands of oak were unlikely to exist in the immediate area.[12]

A conjectural interpretation of the pollen data takes the form of transects away from the River Dee for a time (Fig. 5a) when the hall was functioning, or shortly before it was built, and for a time (Fig. 5b) when the hall was no longer in use. Figure 5a suggests that the edge of the River Dee had a cover of alder and hazel, with some marshland on the landward edge. The immediate vicinity of the site was largely open, with the hall flanked by trampled ground (under grass and ruderals), with cereals and flax grown in arable fields nearby, and with pasture and coppiced hazel beyond. The small amounts of cereal pollen would reflect the fact that the arable fields were not adjacent to the house site. It is not possible to be certain that hazel was coppiced, but there is no reason why it would not have been and charred hazel nut shells were found during the excavation.

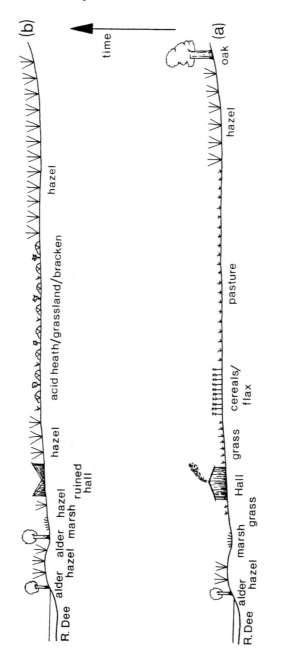

Figure 5: Schematic reconstruction of vegetation transects away from the River Dee at the Balbridie site: (a) for a time when the hall was functioning, or shortly before it was built; (b) for a time when the hall was no longer in use.

Figure 5b presents a rather different vegetational landscape. Alder and hazel have spread into the marshy zone and hazel has spread into areas previously under grass. Land once devoted to arable and adjacent pasture is now dominated by heather, acid grassland and bracken (*Pteridium aquilinum*). There is thus a change from a relatively fertile landscape of mixed farming, to one of rough grazing and/or abandonment. Whether such a transformation was occasioned by agricultural misuse or largely natural processes of soil impoverishment or attendant climatic deterioration is unknown. What is clear is that a substantial timber hall would have required a large supply of oak; clearance of woodland was necessary to provide land for fields and pasture; and after some time, soils became poorer (changing from acid brown earths to podzols [where bases and organic compounds are leached from the upper horizons]) and pastures more rank.

A study of lake sites from across the British Isles[13] has shown that over half of the 15 Scottish lochs experiencing an accelerated erosion of sediments into their basins did so during the Neolithic. This is almost certainly reflecting the inputs of soil erosion probably induced by agricultural activity. In other words, the first and even minor woodland reductions and farming practices resulted in landscape degradation.

MAJOR WOODLAND REDUCTION, SOILS, AND THE PERSISTENCE OF AGRICULTURE

Subsequent to these first reductions in the woodland cover of Scotland, and, of course, in those areas where there was a restoration of tree cover (because of abandonment or because soils permitted it), sustained falls in arboreal taxa began to occur *ca* 4200-3050 14C yr BP (2800-1350 cal BC);[14] and see Fig. 3 where major fall begins at *ca* 3600 14C yr BP [1970 cal BC]). These arboreal declines occur largely within the Bronze and Iron Ages. While they may reflect the advent of metals as efficient materials for axe manufacture, they are as likely to denote the expansion of population and the extension of cleared land. More sites are needed to confirm these patterns; it should be noted that the earlier portion of this timespan covers the period of climate change which also saw the decimation of pine populations as discussed above (cf. Fig. 4). Once again, disentangling the human and the natural is a complex problem.

Were it not for the environmental record, it might be conjectured that the surviving archaeological remains of the Bronze and Iron Ages have obliterated or obscured signs of equally extensive Neolithic occupation. As it is, it seems that the later periods of prehistory and the early historic period not only witnessed an extension of occupation, as confirmed by the palynological records, but also a deterioration in environmental conditions. People also continued to survive, if not thrive. How was this managed? In so far as soils represent the medium in which crops grow, it may be that some answers should be sought from pedology.

Acid soils dominate the present-day distributions in Scotland with peaty soils covering 50.0 per cent of the country and podzols another 11.0 per cent.[15] Brown forest soils, which are superior agriculturally, comprise some 13.9 per cent. The usefulness of soils, however, depends also on such factors as climate, slope, wetness, stoniness and depth. Maps of land capability[15,16] allow for such factors and demonstrate that land now deemed suitable for agriculture is limited to about 28 per cent of Scotland, and is especially located in the Midland Valley and the east coast lowlands. If criteria are narrowed to estimates of land capable of growing a very wide range of crops, however, then only 1.4 per cent of Scotland is considered suitable because of the restrictions imposed by soil quality and climate.[17]

These assessments pertain to present-day patterns, of course, but the underlying assumptions are based on more or less (semi)-permanent land characteristics (e.g. accumulated temperatures, soil moisture deficit, soil depth). As Davidson and Carter[15] point out, however, human responses in the past may have been different from those of today – small patches of land and steep slopes, for example, could be tackled by the ard, allowing areas to be cultivated which would be quite unsuitable for the tractor. Many areas of improved or rough grazing (67 per cent of the country), contain abundant prehistoric and historic settlement remains and attest to the former acceptability of such lands for cultivation.

Evidence from buried soils[18] shows that podzolisation may have been occurring prior to the local inception of agriculture, and proxy evidence from lake sediments and palynology[19] suggests that acidification and peat development had equally early beginnings. In some circumstances there may be an association with Mesolithic activity,[20] but natural soil change as a result of progressive climate and vegetation change is as likely to be implicated. The removal of woodland following natural processes or anthropogenic pressures would encourage leaching, podzolisation, heather colonisation, acidification and peat growth.

In the drier east of the country especially, it seems that soils switched from having profiles recognisable as brown forest soils to iron podzols, and *vice versa*, as land went in and out of cultivation.[15] The act of tillage would promote better drainage and there would be the addition of nutrients from crop residues. Throughout prehistory, it must be supposed that fields were manured naturally (e.g. by animal waste and domestic midden refuse) or intentionally by spreading dung and organic refuse over fields, including ash, animal bedding [peat, heather and grass turves] and seaweed, as was done into historical times in Shetland.[21] Soil micromorphology shows that this was taking place on prehistoric landscapes at Tofts Ness, Sanday, Orkney[22] and at Scord of Brouster, Mainland, Shetland.[23] At the latter site, barley cultivation led to soil erosion on the sloping fields, stoniness increased in upslope areas, and hearth ash and other organic residues were probably employed in an attempt to counteract the impact of cultivation.

Soil erosion was often so severe that not only did accelerated lake sedimentation occur, but radiocarbon dates from sediment cores start to go into reverse up-profile (i.e. they become older) at a number of Scottish sites, especially after *ca* 1800 14C yr BP (200 cal AD).[13,24] This indicates that soil removal was drastic and that the erosional inputs comprised increasingly older soils containing large amounts of old carbon. Increased erosion may have gone hand-in-hand with the use of the iron coulter and deeper ploughing. Yet, at the same time, it would appear that agriculture was sustained for many centuries beyond these impacts – indeed, often continuing to the present day.

The growth of birch, common bent (*Agrostis capillaris*) and sheep's-fescue (*Festuca ovina*) grasses on acid soils and moorland can, it has been estimated, reverse soil acidification within 50-100 years.[25] Similar effects have been posited[26] for birch and holly (*Ilex aquifolium*) communities. Such processes may have occurred accidentally in the past. Heavy grazing can promote the spread of grasses; the cessation of grazing often leads to birch colonisation as can be seen now, for instance, on the Muir of Dinnet National Nature Reserve, Aberdeenshire. It is easy to see how both could occur cyclically over any landscape in time, providing an antidote to soil acidification, although concomitant practices (e.g. plaggening – see below) may negate this effect. Woodland management for the production of coppice woodland in particular, and with a natural 'fallow' understorey of herbs, may well have enabled soils to recover sufficiently to restore some of their fertility. This is not to deny the fact that for upland areas (above around 300 m which is the altitude around which intensive agriculture stops in Scotland), agriculture was never going to be an easy passport to a leisurely existence and by 1988, 41 per cent of Scotland had some heather cover indicating some soil degradation.[17]

WOODLAND AND TIMBER

As we move from prehistoric to historic times, the quality of our information does not necessarily improve. We are still dependent on palynology to reveal that when the Romans arrived the Lowlands were already largely bereft of much of their original forest and the Highlands also perhaps no more afforested than today;[27] the same technique reveals that in Fife extended Roman occupation was accompanied, at least in the Black Loch catchment, by reafforestation, as though the invaders had disrupted a long-established pattern of farming.[7] Palynology, however, has comparatively little to tell us about the Middle Ages, though we need not doubt that the retreat, and occasional temporary re-advance, of woodland was as characteristic of that period as of earlier millennia. We sense that there was no more wood in the early Middle Ages than later; in the south, the Border abbeys intensified sheep production, and land that had once raised pork on acorns in an oakwood now raised wool on open grasslands;[28] everywhere, there is gradual increase in complaints that large timber is hard to find. Ambitious building projects from around AD 1500, whether of hammer-beam roofs like that at Stirling Castle, or of great warships like James IVs *Great Michael,* begin to use imported wood in addition to traditional Scottish sources for large oak, such as Darnaway Forest in Morayshire.[29] By the sixteenth and seventeenth centuries there is a very well established trade in Scandinavian wood, which reveals not so much that Scotland is bereft of woods as that surviving resources can no longer meet the full range of needs of burghs, nobles and kings.[30]

The first quantitative estimate of woodland cover in Scotland becomes possible only with Roy's military survey, undertaken around 1750: then perhaps 4 per cent of the country was under wood, a statistic that scarcely varied in a series of estimates made in the nineteenth century, though this figure came to include an increasing proportion of plantations in place of semi-natural wood.[31] This was one of the lowest percentages of woodland cover in Europe, and already attained before the advent of industrialisation. Why it was so low in Scotland, compared to, say, Denmark or France, or even southern England, is an interesting question. Part of the explanation may be the abundance of alternative fuel in the shape of peat and coal, so that there was less need to husband wood so carefully. Partly it may have to do with climate, the extreme oceanicity of which, at least in the west, hampered regeneration and assisted leaching, peat formation and the natural formation of podsols. Partly it may have to do with inadequate management regimes. There is some evidence that the traditional pre-industrial management, exercised through the baron court and the souming (or rationing) of stock per peasant holding, could not cope with changing external parameters, such as population growth and climate change.[32] Also, the keeping of larger numbers of stock on the hill – horses, cattle, sheep and perhaps in particular goats (which were very abundant in the Highlands around 1700) must have become substantially easier once the wolf had been exterminated in the seventeenth century.

CLIMATE EFFECTS

It is interesting (and perhaps surprising) for us to realise that climate change was one of the biggest environmental challenges that our ancestors had to confront between the late Middle Ages and the mid-nineteenth century, even though they were hardly able to recognise and conceptualise it in these terms. Their problem was not global warming but global cooling, the Little Ice Age, a drop perhaps of 2°C between the thirteenth century and its nadir in the seventeenth century, the worst periods being between around 1580 and 1650, but with no clear recovery until after 1850.[33] Scotland was perhaps peculiarly susceptible, as a mountainous country on the European edge, and some of its effects are quite clear. Cereal cultivation at high altitudes around settlements on the Lammermuirs became impossible;[34] the incidence of famine was exceptionally high between the mid-sixteenth and the mid-seventeenth century, with another famous and serious dearth in the 1690s associated with snowy springs and early autumn frosts.[35] Other effects of climate change are hard to disentangle from anthropogenic factors. In a number of pinewoods from Wester Ross to Argyll, between around 1580 and 1730, there are signs of young trees failing to regenerate in old woods, and the disappearance of mature trees being followed by the irreversible spread of peat, or at least by moorland replacing woodland. Felling episodes, as in the case of Glen Orchy, might precipitate this; in other cases, as at Little Loch Broom, the collapse of the trees seems to have been a purely natural process.[32] It is anyone's guess as to how far the subsequent failure of pines to regenerate was due to grazing pressure or the increasingly favourable natural environment on the ground, or to both operating in conjunction.

SOIL AND FERTILITY

There is a wider question of soil deterioration before the eighteenth century, which is equally difficult to solve. Both in the Scottish uplands and islands, on sites where soil quality in historic time has been generally bad, and in the Lowlands where much of it has been better, enormous human effort went on during the pre-industrial centuries to maintain grain-growing ground in a state of fertility. It was successful enough to allow Scotland to support about a million people around 1700, 90 per cent of them rural. The population is thought to have been higher earlier in that century, but that figure was itself evidently substantially higher than two centuries before when it was still recovering from late medieval declines assumed to be associated with the fourteenth-century plague pandemic. Whether at one million it exceeded the medieval maximum, or even the figure at the time of the Roman invasion, is simply not known.[35,36,37]

Methods of soil fertilisation known as 'plaggen', such as described for Papa Stour and elsewhere in the Northern Isles[21,38] were widespread from at least the Middle Ages until the mid-eighteenth century, and in places still practised until the start of the twentieth century. At Papa Sour this involved stripping part of the outfield of turf, mixing the latter with seaweed, dung and ashes, and spreading it to maintain fertility on an infield kept under constant cultivation for oats or that primitive form of barley known in Scotland as bere. In the long term, this must have redistributed nutrients around the farm settlement, enriching one area by impoverishing another, and perhaps undermining the ability of the grazing land to support as many cattle as before and this to produce the dung that was a still more vital input to the arable land. In other words, it was of questionable sustainability.

AGRICULTURAL IMPROVEMENT

Although Scottish agriculture before the Union of the Parliaments was not incapable of innovation and change,[36,39] that it was of low productivity compared to elsewhere was obvious to commentators of all political persuasions.[40] It is possible, as has been argued for Denmark,[41] that centuries of shallow ploughing in a wet climate had led to a deterioration in the accessible soil that contemporary manuring techniques could not counteract. In the half-century after 1760 there took place in Scotland, as indeed in Denmark, what can unquestionably be described as an agricultural revolution:[42] in both countries the key innovation was probably the introduction of clover as a nitrogen fixing crop, along with improved ploughing techniques and in Scotland's case, by the use of lime and marl on an enormous scale to counter acidification. Rising production allowed a doubling of population to about 2 million by 1821 without any great recourse to food imports (Table 1). Much of the population increment was released from agricultural production and formed the work-force for the concomitant and equally dramatic Industrial Revolution, in its first phase almost entirely based on textiles.[43] Though towns grew greatly, much textile production was still rural based in 1820.

Scottish farming continued to increase in efficiency and reputation throughout the first half of the Victorian period: foreigners came from far and wide to visit the Lothians, and a weighty agronomist literature gave advice to a literate and educated class of tenants, as well as to their landlords.[44,45,46] It was a golden age for agricultural self-sufficiency and organic farming, and Lowland Scotland had the most sophisticated systems of rotation, manuring and implement technology in the world. It is a memorable experience to walk round the remains of one of the great Victorian steadings of East Lothian or Berwickshire today and see the cattle sheds where stock was fed in winter from wagons that ran on rails from the turnip store, and note the arrangements for the dung to be shovelled out and taken to the fields, and the impressive smoke-stack topping a furnace once fed with a mixture of coal, straw and chaff to drive the belts of the threshing engines. There is no part of our built heritage less appreciated than these monuments of High Farming; most will disappear, though many are now being carefully recorded for posterity by the Royal Commission[47] (Fig. 6).

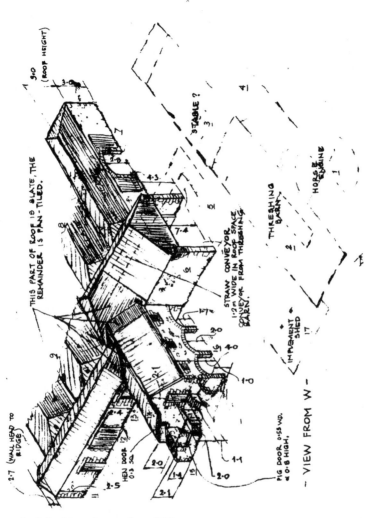

Figure 6: A Lothians factory farm (48).

Not until after 1870 was there much recourse either to food imports or to artificial fertilisers, and such was the flexibility and specialisation of Scottish farmers of this era that there was little sign of the so-called agricultural depression that affected the south of England. Concentration on, for example, dairy production for the cities and quality meat from Aberdeen Angus herds saw off the worst problems of falling incomes until after the First World War, when there was, quite briefly, a decade or so of real agricultural depression.[46]

After the Second World War, the subsidised chemicalisation and mechanisation of farming produced big increases in output and income, though at a heavy cost to biodiversity and rural employment (to say nothing of the quality of food) which its apologists consider inevitable. Only now, with average farming incomes slumping back in real terms to below what they were in the 1930s,[49] can Scottish farming be said to be facing the prospect of long-term depression and structural decline. At present the pain is unequally divided, with upland farms very much worse off than lowland ones. But the viability of chemical farming itself on some of the most fertile soils of the east coast is being questioned by the extent of nitrate overload on the river systems, beginning (but not ending) with the Ythan catchment.

TOWN AND COUNTRY

There is a welcome political mood afoot in contemporary Scotland, through land reform and in other ways, to empower local rural communities. Nevertheless, one of the lessons of the last two centuries that it would be unwise to overlook is the degree to which the economic needs and social customs of urban communities have come to determine the life of the countryside. Before 1700, when nine out of ten Scots lived in small rural settlements of a few hundred or less, the degree of local empowerment was very large, albeit mainly vested in the laird for economic purposes and in a self-appointed kirk session for moral ones. There was of course trade in the local market, but much of it rural exchange, such as Highlanders swapping cattle, skins, timber and peats for the Lowlanders' oatmeal and malt. Equally there was external political disturbance, depending on the twists and turns of kings and kirks. But for most of the time and for most purposes what happened in the burgh was of small account to the local ferm-toun.

Already in the eighteenth-century this was rapidly changing. The demand of Sheffield and other producers for high-grade iron impelled the Duke of Argyll and his neighbours for the first time to fence their oakwoods against their tenants' stock, and to turn woods over to production of coppice charcoal, cut sustainably on twenty-year rotations. Contrariwise, graziers in Inverness-shire supplying the Smithfield market were accused of threatening by overgrazing the young trees on the hillsides, what a contemporary in 1784 described as the 'thick stool of oak [which] appears among the heath over great part of that extensive moor which is situated between Fort William and the River Spey'.[28] Meanwhile, grain was freely moved from the east coast by boat, including canal boat, to feed the city of Glasgow. Edinburgh supplied rural parishes like Corstorphine and Newington with enough human dung to keep them under constant wheat cultivation to provide it with white flour, a very perfect example of recycling. As rural incomes rose, country tastes for the products of the new manufactories was led by town fashion. The local ministers in the 1790s deplored in the pages of the *Statistical Account* the luxurious tendencies of a population dressing in cotton, but wrung their hands in vain.

Until the middle of the nineteenth century, the countryside had bargaining power, in that it formed a substantial part of the town's market, and the political balance of power, even after the 1832 Reform Act, was still heavily skewed to the rich in rural constituencies. Thereafter, however, urban population grew rapidly, while the rural population in Highland and Lowland alike fell inexorably, and political power slipped to the middle class and the working class of the towns by successive reform acts of 1868, 1884-5 and 1918. The population of Scotland stood at 4.7 million by 1911 and the markets for its labour – ships, steel, coal, jute, tweed – lay mainly abroad. More and more of its food came to be imported. In the twentieth century, population growth lessened and dependence on international markets became a real problem, but Scotland still became more urban and more prosperous, basing its economy increasingly on services and on inter-British and inter-European trade[43] (Tables 2 and 3).

As the countryside became more marginal to the town, the manner in which the town determined all the critical changes in the countryside became even more pronounced. In the nineteenth century, the Highlands fell victim to the clearances because the Lowland manufacturing towns needed the wool and the meat of the Cheviot and the Blackface sheep. If there had been isolated complaints about overgrazing before, by the 1880s they were becoming universal in the north.[50] When, at about that time, sheep farms were becoming supplemented and replaced by deer farms and grouse moors, it was to meet the consequences of a falling price for wool in the face of imports, and a rising demand for sport in wild places from the urban rich. In the twentieth century, the experience of urban shortages in the face of wartime blockades led to a new concern about the countryside. The Forestry Commission was established after the First World War, and under its guidance and with the help of subsidy and tax-break, the amount of ground under wood grew from about five per cent to the present 19 per cent of the land surface. The Second World War and subsequent economic difficulties led to the widespread use of agricultural subsidy, with, eventually, concomitant overproduction and ecological damage. In the 1990s, a European Union and a British government increasingly focused on globalisation and the virtues of free trade and low taxes is trying to rid itself of the incubus of keeping domestic agricultural production at earlier levels, with further changes inevitable.

Not one of these momentous developments originated in the countryside (except, possibly, the inspiration for the Forestry Commission). Some were forced on rural communities, others embraced by them, but the great thrusts for changes in land use came from urban demand and urban priorities. Also, it is worth emphasising the degree to which rural depopulation was a choice of country people not because they were forced off the land but because they found the town more rewarding:[51] as one historian has put it 'urbanisation meant more jobs, a wider diversity of social contacts and infinitely greater colour and excitement in the lives of the masses'.[52] The first generation, in many cases at least, was only too glad to leave; those herded aboard ships and beholding the Hebrides in dreams were very much the minority.

As the countryside became unfamiliar, it also became more attractive for a visit, for those with leisure and money.[53] The tourist was initially the fastidious, well-heeled connoisseur, like William Wordsworth, Thomas MacCulloch and Walter Scott, who developed the theory of what was good landscape – the wild, the picturesque, the sublime – with which we all now mostly agree. In the nineteenth century, the romantic was joined by the sportsman, the alpine climber, the rambler and the delicate visitor to the hydropathic hotels. In the twentieth century, it became mass-tourism with the addition of the skier, the bird-watcher, the youth hosteller, the family renting a holiday cottage and above all the motorist. Quite suddenly it became a leading Scottish industry (accounting for around five per cent of GNP), more valuable than agriculture (less than two per cent).

The urban visitors knew what they liked about the countryside, and they were prepared to pay for it. Unfortunately, those whom they paid were seldom those who suffered the consequences of their preferences. It was the Speyside bed-and-breakfast owner who took their money, the local crofter whose cows strayed when they left the gates open. It was the Islay farmers who suffered the depredations of the spectacular numbers of geese who drew the birdwatchers who paid the ferry company, the garage owner and the village supermarket.

SOME CONCLUDING POINTS

The other contributions will be replete with terms such as competition, economic drivers, efficiency, policy instruments, public values and agendas. We may only be able to glimpse such factors dimly, especially for the distant past, but the historical record has the ability to satisfy a thirst for knowledge with some chance of answering questions about 'where', 'why', and 'how'.

We have not shown there to be a clear agenda in prehistory – though claims for such may be made by those who feel that organisation sufficient to construct ritual monuments (e.g. Callanish, Cleaven Dyke, Ring of Brodgar or hundreds of other circles), or to manage pragmatically a rural landscape without warfare[54] constitutes social control, or that the lack of an agenda also constitutes an agenda. By the time that we reach the late 18th century AD, the Improvers were enacting an agenda aimed at improving agricultural efficiency by land management and agro-technology, but this was as much for the benefit of the landowner as for the tenant farmer or the crofter. The activities of owner and crofter alike, however, assisted in maintaining the open landscapes which characterise most of Scotland today.

Of vital concern to us as researchers of the past is the stewardship of our raw materials. Peat extraction, lake drainage and the destruction of archaeological sites (by natural means, such as faunal activity and erosion, as well as by developers and even archaeologists) is denuding the potential research resource base. Caesium-137 estimates of soil loss through plough-ing of one important archaeological site in Perthshire[55] reveals an erosion rate of 0.5 mm per annum since 1953 and this may be an underestimate.[56] Many cropmark sites (cf. Balbridie above) could be at risk of irremediable damage or complete loss within a few decades, a situation exacerbated by more intensive cropping since 1945 and a recent pattern of increased winter rainfall.[57] The loss of peat, lake sediments and soils not only prevents us from investigating the past using currently-known methods, but also means that such media are unavailable to posterity as new techniques become available or as we begin to investigate entities as yet under-appreciated or unknown. A stronger alliance between Scottish Natural Heritage and Historic Scotland in respect of such heritage concerns should surely be seen as a priority,[58] lest future generations are to be denied access to their reconstructible past.

In the last century and a half we have become an urban people. Most tax-payers live in towns, and in the twentieth century tax payments to government have come to stand at some 40 per cent of GNP. It is inescapable that we will get the kind of countryside that we are prepared to pay for, and that the countryside will need to be paid for, one way or another. The principle of no taxation without representation, first reluctantly brought to the attention of the British government by the eighteenth-century Americans, will inevitably limit the extent of rural empowerment. Those who live in towns may feel that their financial contribution to the countryside (including an average farm subsidy in Scotland of £26,000 per annum), justifies a right to decide that a fox hunt, a seal cull or a coniferous forest is inappropriate – it is not ignorance, it is preference. And those urban people who want a beautiful rural locality preserved for their pleasure have a right to be heard as clearly as those who argue that its destruction would provide local jobs. These facts are part of the logic of history since the Industrial Revolution, and must put certain appropriate limits to rural empowerment.

Table 1:   Growth of Scottish Population (millions)

1707	1.0
1755	1.3
1801	1.6
1821	2.1
1841	2.6
1861	3.0
1881	3.7
1901	4.5
1921	4.8
1951	5.1
1971	5.2
1991	5.1

Source: Flinn (1977) and censuses

Table 2:   Transition to an urban Scotland

Percentage of total population in centres of 5,000 or over:

1801	21.0
1811	24.2
1821	27.5
1831	31.2
1841	32.7
1851	35.9
1861	39.4
1871	44.4
1881	48.9
1891	53.5
1901	57.6
1911	58.6
1921	61.3
1931	63.1
1951	64.0

Percentage of total population in centres of 1,000 or over

1861	57.6
1901	74.3
1931	80.1
1951	82.2

Source: Flinn (1977)

Table 3:   Transition away from agriculture in Scotland

Percentage of employed population engaged in agriculture in Scotland

1851	24.9
1871	22.2
1891	14.0
1911	10.6
1931	9.0
1951	7.3
1971	4.1
1991	1.5

Source: Lee (1979) and censuses

ACKNOWLEDGEMENTS

We would like to thank Professors Ian Ralston and Graeme Whittington, of the Universities of Edinburgh and St Andrews respectively, for their comments on an earlier draft of this paper.

REFERENCES

1. M Bell and M J C Walker, *Late Quaternary environmental change: physical and human perspectives,* London, 1992.
   K J Edwards and I B M Ralston eds, *Scotland: Environment and Archaeology, 8000 BC-AD 1000,* Chichester, 1997a.
   K J Edwards and J P Sadler eds, *Holocene Environments of Prehistoric Britain (Journal of Quaternary Science [Quaternary Proceedings])* 7, 1999.
   J J Lowe and C J M Walker eds, Reconstructuring Quaternary Environments, 2nd edition, London 1997.

2. G J Barclay, 'The Neolithic', in K J Edwards and I B M Ralston, eds, *Scotland: Environment and Archaeology, 8000 BC-AD 1000,* Chichester (1997) 127–149.
   A S Henshall Scottish chambered tombs and long mounds', C Renfrew, ed, British pre-history: *A new outline,* London (1974), 137–164.

3. K J Edwards and I B M Ralston, 'Environment and people in prehistoric and early historical times: preliminary considerations', in Edwards, K J and Ralston, I B M eds, *Scotland: Environment and Archaeology: 8000 BC-AD 1000,* Chichester (1997b), 1–10.

4. F McCormick and P C Buckland, 'The vertebrate fauna', in K J Edwards and I B M Ralston eds, *Scotland: Environment and Prehistory, 8000 BC-AD 1000,* Chichester (1997), 84–103.

5. K J Edwards 'A Mesolithic of the Western and Northern Isles of Scotland? Evidence from pollen and charcoal', in Pollard, T and Morrison, A eds, *The early prehistory of Scotland,* Edinburgh (1996), 23–38.

6. K J Edwards, K R Hirons and P J Newell, 'The palaeoecological and prehistoric context of minerogenic layers in blanket peat: a study from Loch Dee, southwest Scotland', *The Holocene* 1 (1991), 29–39.
   K R Hirons and K J Edwards 'Pollen and related studies at Kinloch, Isle of Rhum, Scotland, with particular reference to possible early human impacts on vegetation. *New Phytologist* 116 (1990), 715–727.

7. G Whittington, K J Edwards and P R Cundill, 'Late- and post-glacial vegetational change at Black Loch, Fife, eastern Scotland – a multiple core approach', *New Phytologist* 118 (1991), 147–166.

8. B Huntley and H J B Birks, *An Atlas of Past and Present Pollen Maps for Europe: 0–13000 Years Ago,* Cambridge, 1983.

9. B A Brayshay and K J Edwards, 'Lateglacial and Holocene vegetational history of South Uist and Barra', in Gilbertson, D D, Kent, M and Grattan, J P eds, *The Outer Hebrides: the Last 14,000 Years,* Sheffield (1996), 13–26.

10. K D Bennett, 'The Post-Glacial history of *Pinus sylvestris* in the British Isles', in *Quaternary Science Reviews* 3 (1984), 133–156.
    A D Dubois and D K Ferguson, 'The climatic history of pine in the Cairngorms based on radiocarbon dates and stable isotope analysis, with an account of the events leading up to its colonization', *Review of Palaeobotany and Palynology* 46 (1985), 55–80.

11. A D Fairweather and I B M Ralston, 'The Neolithic timber hall at Balbridie, Grampian Region, Scotland: a preliminary note on dating and plant macrofossils', *Antiquity* 67 (1993), 313–323.

12. K J Edwards, 'Palynological studies at Balbridie' in Ralston, I B M, *Excavations of a Neolithic Timber Hall at Balbridie Farm, Banchory- Ternan, Aberdeenshire,* Department of Archaeology, University of Edinburgh, Monograph Series, forthcoming.

13. K J Edwards and G Whittington, 'Lake sediments, palaeoenvironments and human impact in prehistoric and historical times', *Catena.* (forthcoming).

14. K J Edwards and G Whittington, 'Vegetation history', in Edwards, K J and Ralston, I B M eds, *Scotland: Environment and Archaeology: 8000 BC-AD 1000,* Chichester (1997), 63–82.

15. D A Davidson and S P Carter, 'Soils and their evolution', in Edwards, K J and Ralston, I B M, *Scotland: Environment and Archaeology, 8000 BC-AD 1000,* Chichester, (1997), 45–62.

16. J S Bibby, H A Douglas, A J Thomasson and J S Robertson, *Land Capability Classification for Agriculture,* Monograph of the Soil Survey of Scotland, Macaulay Institute for Soil Research, Aberdeen, 1982.

17. J Miles, 'The soil resource and problems today; an ecologist's perspective', in Foster, S and Smout, T C eds, *The History of Soils and Fields,* Aberdeen (1994), 145–158.

18. R P J McCullagh and R Tipping eds, *The Lairg Project 1988–1996. The Evolution of an Archaeological Landscape in Northern Scotland,* Scottish Trust for Archaeological Research Monograph 3, 1998.

19. K J Edwards, G Whittington and K R Hirons, 'The relationship between fire and long-term wet heath development in South Uist, Outer Hebrides, Scotland', in Thompson, D B A, Hestor, A J and Usher, M B eds, *Heaths and moorland: cultural landscapes,* Edinburgh (1995), 240–248.
    W Pennington, E Y Haworth, A P Bonny and J P Lishman, 'Lake sediments in northern Scotland', *Philosophical Transactions of the Royal Society of London* B264 (1972), 191–294.

20. G W Dimbleby, *The Development of British Heathlands and their Soils,* Oxford Forestry Memoir 23, 1962.

21. B E Crawford and B Ballin Smith, *The Biggings, Papa Stour, Shetland: the History and Archaeology of a Royal Norwegian Farm,* Society of Antiquaries of Scotland Monograph Series No. 15, Edinburgh, 1999.
    A Fenton, *The Northern Isles: Orkney and Shetland,* Edinburgh, 1978.

22. S J Dockrill, J M Bond, A Milles, I Simpson and J Ambers, 'Tofts Ness, Sanday, Orkney. An integrated study of a buried Orcadian landscape', in Luff, R and Rowley-Conwy, P eds, *Whither Environmental Archaeology?,* Oxford (1994), 115–132.

23. A Whittle, M Keith-Lucas, A Milles, B Noddle, S Rees and J C C Romans, *Scord of Brouster: an Early Agricultural Settlement on Shetland. Excavations 1977–1979.* Oxford University Committee for Archaeology Monograph No. 9, 1986.

24. K J Edwards and I B M Ralston, 'Environment and archaeology in Scotland: some observations', in Edwards, K J and Ralston, I B M eds, *Scotland: Environment and Archaeology: 8000 BC-AD 1000,* Chichester (1997c), 255–266.
    K J Edwards and K M Rowntree, 'Radiocarbon and palaeoenvironmental evidence for changing rates of erosion at a Flandrian stage site in Scotland', in Cullingford, R A, Davidson, D A and Lewin J. eds, *Timescales in geomorphology,* Chichester (1980), 207–223.

25. J Miles, 'Vegetation and soil change in the uplands', in Usher, M B and Thompson, D B eds, *Ecological Change in the Uplands*, Oxford (1988), 57–70.

26. G W Dimbleby, 'Pollen analysis', in Brothwell, D and Higgs, E eds, *Science in Archaeology*, 2nd edn, London (1969), 167–177.

27. D J Breeze, *Roman Scotland*, London, 1996.
R Tipping, 'The form and fate of Scotland's woodlands', *Proceedings of the Society of Antiquaries of Scotland* 124 (1994), 1–54.

28. T C Smout, 'Woodland history before 1850', in Smout T C ed., *Scotland Since Prehistory, Natural Change and Human Impact*, Aberdeen (1993), 40–49.

29. A Crone and R Fawcett, 'Dendrochronology, documents and the timber trade: new evidence for the building history of Stirling castle, Scotland', in *Medieval Archaeology* 42 (1998), 68–87.
J Gilbert, *Hunting and Hunting Reserves in Medieval Scotland*, Edinburgh, 1979.

30. Anon (ed.), *Timber and Trade: Articles on the Timber Export from the Ryfylke-area to Scotland and Holland in the 16th and 17th Century*, N.p. Lokalhistorisk Stiftelse, fagrapport, nr.1., Tysver, Norway, 1999.
A Lillehammer, 'The Scottish-Norwegian timber trade in the Stavanger area in the sixteenth and seventeenth centuries', in Smout, T C ed., *Scotland and Europe 1200–1850*, Edinburgh (1986).

31. M L Anderson, *A History of Scottish Forestry*, Edinburgh, 1967.
A C O'Dell, 'A view of Scotland in the middle of the eighteenth century', *Scottish Geographical Magazine* 69 (1953), 58–63.

32. T C Smout and F Watson, 'Exploiting semi-natural woods, 1600–1800', in Smout, T.C. ed., *Scottish Woodland History*, Edinburgh (1997), 86–100.

33. J A Grove, *The Little Ice Age*, London, 1988.

34. M L Parry, 'Secular climate change and marginal agriculture', *Transactions of the Institute of British Geographers* 64 (1975), 1–14.

35. M W Flinn ed, *Scottish Population History from the Seventeenth Century to the 1930s*, Cambridge, 1977.

36. R A Dodgshon, *Land and Society in Early Scotland*, Oxford, 1981.

37. I D Whyte, *Scotland Before the Industrial Revolution: an Economic and Social History, c.1050–c.1750*, London, 1995.

38. D A Davidson and I A Simpson, 'Soils and landscape history: case studies from the northern Isles of Scotland' in Foster S and Smout T C eds, *The History of Soils and Field Systems*, Aberdeen, (1994), 66–74.

39. I D Whyte, *Agriculture and Society in Seventeenth-Century Scotland*. Edinburgh, 1979

40. J E Handley, *Scottish Farming in the Eighteenth Century*, London, 1953. Henshall, A S, 'Scottish chambered tombs and long mounds', in Renfrew, C ed, *British prehistory: a new outline*, London (1974), 137–164.

41. T Kjærgaard, *The Danish Revolution, 1500–1800: an Ecohistorical Interpretation*, Cambridge, 1994. Lee, C H, *British Regional Employment Statistics 1841–1971*, Cambridge, 1979.

42. T M Devine, *The Transformation of Rural Scotland*, Edinburgh, 1994.

43. T M Devine, *The Scottish Nation: 1700–2000*, London, 1999.

44. T C Smout, *A History of the Scottish People 1560–1830*, London, 1969.

45. A G Bradley, *When Squires and Farmers Thrived*, London, 1927.

46. J A Symon, *Scottish Farming Past and Present,* Edinburgh, 1959.

47. RCAHMS, *Scottish Farm Buildings Survey. 1: East Central Scotland. 2: Orkney.* Royal Commission on the Ancient and Historical Monuments of Scotland and National Museums of Scotland, Edinburgh, 1998.

48. Anon., 'Designs of farm builldings, drawn up under the direction of a committee of Highland Society of Scotland', *Prize Essays and Transactions of the Royal Highland and Agricultural Society of Scotland* New Series 2 (1831), 365–390.

49. K Blaxter and N Robertson, *From Dearth to Plenty: the Modern Revolution in Food Production,* Cambridge, 1995.

50. J Hunter, 'Sheep and deer: Highland sheep farming 1850–1900', *Northern Scotland* 1 (1973), 199–222.

51. T C Smout, *A Century of the Scottish People,* London, 1986.

52. A S Wohl, *Endangered Lives,* London, 1983.

53. T C Smout, 'Tours in the Scottish highlands from the eighteenth to the twentieth century', *Northern Scotland* 5 (1983), 99–121.

54. S Foster and T C Smout eds, *The History of Soils and Field Systems,* Aberdeen, 1994.

55. G J Barclay and G S Maxwell, *The Cleaven Dyke and Littleour: Monuments in the Neolithic of Tayside,* Society of Antiquaries of Scotland Monograph Series No. 13, Edinburgh, 1998.

56. D A Davidson, I C Grieve, A N Tyler, G J Barclay and G S Maxwell, 'Archaeological sites: assessment of erosion risk', in *Journal of Archaeological Science* 25 (1998), 857–860.

57. D A Davidson and D J Harrison, 'Water erosion on arable land in Scotland: results of an erosion survey', in *Soil Use and Management* 11 (1995), 63–68.

58. K Edwards and I B M Ralston, 'Environment and archaeology in Scotland: some observations', in K J Edwards and I B M Ralston eds, *Scotland: Environment and Archaeology: 8000 BC-AD 1000,* Chichester (1997), 255–266.

2

The Environment and Land Use of the Future

T J Maxwell and M G R Cannell

INTRODUCTION

TO MAKE PREDICTIONS about land use and the environment of the future requires an analysis of our current understanding of the primary factors that are likely to influence and bring about change. These factors include those related to policy and the goal-seeking behaviour of the Scottish people as reflected in and determined by the EU, UK and Scottish legislatures. In addition, change arising from changes in biophysical and biogeochemical processes brought about by climate change will also be important. Land use change in Scotland will be determined largely by the relative and absolute economic performance of agriculture and forestry and the operational guidelines and/or statutory controls put in place to protect the environment, the welfare of animals and the health of people. It will also be determined by the increasing influence of urban dwellers and their more explicit demand for environmental goods and services associated with recreation, sport, tourism and a general enjoyment of the countryside.

LONG-TERM UNCERTAINTY AND THE POTENTIAL USE OF MODELS

Predicting change over a time-period of fifty years, however, is fraught with difficulty. Bearing in mind the complex inter-relationships between bio-physical, social and economic change, it is inevitable that predicting ultimate outcomes will be subject to great uncertainty. However, if it is the intention to manage at least some aspects of change it is necessary at least to try to establish the likely direction of change, if not its absolute extent. History can be informative but not exclusively helpful. It requires to be combined with an understanding and knowledge of the processes that bring about change. There has also to be a healthy acceptance that the complexity of change results in evolutionary and emergent outcomes rather than well-defined blueprints or national plans. It is, therefore, apposite that we were asked briefly to review the extent to which models may be able to provide a more rigorous approach.

Forecasting change using a modeling approach in the context of this paper requires an ability to accommodate two fundamental epistemologies, the positivist view of the physical scientist of an *a priori* given world and the transactional or constructivist position of the social scientist: the social scientist's position being based upon the dynamics of interaction between man and the environment. Land use change happens at the interface between human and biophysical systems. One scientific tradition suggests that it is predictable; another that it is not. There is clearly a cross-disciplinary challenge here.[1] At present models forecasting the future predominantly deal with biophysical parameters, such as those concerned with the impact of climate change, and for the purposes of establishing trends they do so tolerably well. Few deal with the interface between biophysical parameters and social behaviour.

At the level of the farm/estate significant progress is being made in developing decision support tools to assist in the planning, appraisal and evaluation of change with an ability to forecast economic, social and environmental outcomes. The potential complexity of land use options and their impacts in interacting with a range of individual fields on a farm requires an optimising system capable of finding satisfactory multi-objective solutions. One example, LADSS – a land allocation decision support system[1] does just this. It integrates a Geographic Information System, a simulation system and a multi-objective optimising system based on the use of genetic algorithms. The latter enables the generating of a population of land allocations solutions describing the trade-off between, for example, economic and environmental risk. At the local level, this is precisely the kind of information that will be required in the future to aid decisions in managing change.

At the regional and national level many interactions between individuals and organisations need to be considered (eg individual farm households, special interest groups, local government authorities). The relatively new area of science covered by complex system theory has the potential to address exactly this sort of problem. In a complex system the individual entities interact to create emergent properties that cannot readily be deduced from the rule of the behaviour of the individual entities. A well-known example of this is the flocking behaviour of birds.

The modelling approach currently being developed at MLURI[2] provides a Framework for the Environmental Assessment of Regional Land Use Scenarios (FEARLUS). It uses the SWARM agent based modelling environment developed at the Santa Fe Institute.[3] While accepting that the approach is speculative, it could nevertheless represent a more explicit approach to decision making by combining our biophysical understanding with our goal-seeking behaviour often expressed currently through a mixture of concepts (like sustainable development), imitation (doing what one's neighbour does), advocacy and dogma.

As we indicated at the outset, it is unlikely that we will be able to predict change with great certainty. Modelling can, however, be used to contribute more explicitly to the explanation of potential evolutionary and emergent outcomes and provide an intelligent environment through which to develop decisions and manage change. They will doubtless become increasingly important in the future. But for the time being, we will have to rely on the age-old system of postulation, some facts, intuition, instinct, political insight and discussion as being the major tools of the forecaster's trade.

It is therefore important that we state the underlying assumption of this paper. It is that the social and economic drivers of change influencing the management and use of land, and climate will be the significant determinants affecting the future environment of Scotland.

GOAL-SEEKING BEHAVIOUR AND THE FACTORS DETERMINING POLICY DEVELOPMENT

It follows, therefore, that the philosophical context within which the social and economic drivers of change are likely to operate becomes important. In this regard, the development of the concept of sustainability has arguably provided one of the most unifying global paradigms of recent times. It has provided a context within which economic, social and environmental goals can be considered together and debated. Whatever we may think about its effectiveness, it now lies at the heart of European, UK and Scottish policy development. It is likely to provide, for the foreseeable future, the working hypothesis by which a balance is struck in the use of our natural resources between the achievement of environmental and social objectives, and the drive for wealth creation and economic competitiveness.

But the concept of sustainability is not founded on absolutes and over a period of 50 years, we will see change in how society interprets sustainability. Pearce[4] has described a 'sustainability' spectrum which extends from a strongly technocentric to a strongly ecocentric interpretation. The interpretation that seems to most fit current and probable future thinking over the next 50 years, at least in the 'western' world, is that described by Pearce[4] as being 'accommodating'. This suggests that natural resources will increasingly be conserved, protected and enhanced; economic instruments will be used to deliver goods that have been produced in an 'environmentally friendly' way; measures of economic growth will increasingly take account of natural resource use; the concept of infinite substitution of capital is likely to be rejected and the idea of managing capital as a constant will increasingly prevail; the ethical position both globally and locally is likely to be motivated increasingly towards 'caring for others' and satisfying to a greater degree intragenerational and intergenerational equity.

The rate of change within this spectrum, however, will almost certainly depend on the success of the macro-economy and its ability to deliver secure levels of income for the majority of the population. In a Scottish land use context, this means that the extent to which agriculture and forestry remain viable and prosper and the extent to which the environment and our natural heritage is conserved, protected and managed will depend on the willingness of the public to accept that at least a part of their 'disposable' income is used to such ends. But change will also depend upon natural forces which, though affected by our actions, are largely out of our control. Nevertheless, it is important that the consequences of climate change and anthropogenic pollution are understood and considered in relation to the social and economic drivers of change.

CLIMATE CHANGE AND ANTHROPOGENIC POLLUTION

Future trends in climate

It is a fact that the world has warmed by about 0.3C since 1970 and that four of the five warmest years in the 340–year temperature record in England have occurred in the last decade. Globally, 1998 was the warmest year in the 20th century and perhaps in the whole second millennium.[5]

The Intergovernmental Panel on Climate Change[6] concluded that the 'balance of evidence' is that increasing greenhouse gas concentrations are partly responsible for this warming and the 37 nations that met in Kyoto in 1997 accepted that climate change is sufficiently real to curb greenhouse gas emissions. There are, however, large uncertainties about future emissions and their effects on climate as determined by the 'climate sensitivity' of Global Climate Models. Also, the predictions are still at a very coarse resolution. All of Scotland north of the central belt falls within one GCM grid square (2.5 latitude, 3.75 longitude) with an assumed altitude of 221m, so that local climates can be predicted only by using regional climate models or other downscaling methods, which introduce further uncertainty. The future atmospheric pollution climate is similarly uncertain, particularly as cuts in emissions are not necessarily matched by reductions in deposition (eg for sulphate in rain) and future levels of many pollutants depend on climate as well as emission scenarios (eg tropospheric ozone).

Hulme and Jenkins[7] provided a set of UK climate change scenarios based on 1998 predictions from the Meteorological Office model known as HadCM2. Perhaps the best scenario to consider is one they called 'medium high', which assumed a 1% annual growth in greenhouse gas concentrations over the next century – close to the IPCC 'business-as-usual' assumption, giving global warming of 3.1C by the 2080s.

In this scenario, by the 2050s Scotland warms by about 1.6C in summer and 1.8C in winter. Winter precipitation increases by about 10%, with some tendency for increased rainfall in summer. The climate of Aberdeen will come to resemble that of Anglesey now and the west coast of Scotland will have the current climate of the west of Ireland.[8] Throughout the year, but especially in winter, there may be less solar radiation, owing to increased cloud cover, a smaller diurnal range in temperature, with less inter-annual temperature variability, but perhaps more variable rainfall. There is no evidence that mean windspeeds will change appreciably or consistently in any season, in fact normal winter gales may become less frequent, although very severe gales may occur more frequently. It is more likely that increased and more variable rainfall will be accompanied by more frequent intense rainfall events, increasing the risk of flooding. Also, warming will lengthen the growing season, with the number of day-degrees above 5.5C increasing by about 5% per decade.

In this scenario, warming will increase mean sea levels around the UK by about 28 cm by the 2050s, but land rising (isostatic adjustment) in Scotland will reduce the net increase in sea level to about 17 cm in the west and 23 cm in the east.

Gradually, the North Atlantic thermo-haline circulation, which draws the Gulf Stream to Scotland, is likely to weaken owing to the addition of fresh water from melting Arctic ice and warming at northern latitudes. This may already be happening, as evidenced by a drop in salt concentration in North Atlantic surface waters. However, at present the seas around Scotland are warming and the Meteorological Office model, which includes ocean circulation, predicts that any weakening in the North Atlantic circulation in the next 100 years will not prevent Western Europe warming at a rate close to the global average.

Future trends in anthropogenic pollution

There are three major air pollution problems which affect Scottish vegetation: tropospheric ozone, eutrophication owing to N deposition, and acidification due to sulphur, ammonia and nitrogen oxide deposition.

Some consider that the most serious in future is likely to be ozone. It is important to realize that mean ozone concentrations rise with altitude, because higher windspeeds prevent the formation of temperature inversions and night-time depletion to the ground. Consequently, much of the Scottish uplands experiences mean ozone concentrations over 40 ppb in April-September, equal to those in the English lowlands. These concentrations lead to accumulated summertime exposures which have been shown to damage crops and some trees.[9] Also, short-term peaks of 60–80 ppb occur several times each summer over most of Scotland and are known to be damaging to a range of plant species. The prognosis of atmospheric modellers is that mean ozone concentrations, which doubled in the 20th century, will continue to rise in the 21st century. By the 2020s, the threshold of 40ppb may become a common background concentration for much of the summer in Scotland and elsewhere.[10]

The next most important air pollutant is likely to be nitrogen. In high rainfall areas in the Southern Uplands and Southwest Highlands deposition averages 25–30 kg N ha^{-1} a^{-1}, whereas in northern regions with less polluted air, and in the lowlands away from agricultural sources of ammonia, deposition is commonly 5–10 kg N ha^{-1} a^{-1}.[11] N deposition rates are likely to remain high well into the 21st century owing to continued vehicle emissions and livestock agriculture.

The third air pollutant issue is acidification, caused by emissions of sulphur and N oxides. Although S emissions have been reduced in the UK by 25%, deposition in rain and cloud droplets remains high in the Scottish uplands and acidification is still an important issue.[10,12]

Impacts on agriculture and forestry

Managing the impact of climate change on the farm within these limits is unlikely to be difficult. Farmers are well used to the vagaries of weather and to change. There is every indication that the industry will be able to adapt to the threats and opportunities presented by climate change in the next 50 years, as it has to changes of many kinds over the last 50 years, by switching crops or varieties, changing agronomic practices and using irrigation, fertilizers and agrochemicals.[13]

Overall, any effect of climate change may be beneficial for Scottish agriculture, bearing in mind that rainfall levels will be sustained. Most studies predict a small but positive effect of climate change on crop yields, in part due to increasing CO_2 concentrations, but also in response to warming, as evidenced in recent warm years.[14] However, yield predictions are complicated by shifts from spring to winter crops, main crop to early potatoes and by assumptions about irrigation and, of course, prices.[14,15] In time, warming in Scotland may enable farmers to diversify by increasing the range of crops that can be grown profitably, including high value crops such as fodder maize, sugar beet, more oil seed rape and vegetables. It will also enable crops to be grown at higher altitudes. But, at the same time, some of the benefits of cold winters in controlling pests of soft fruit and seed potatoes may be lost.

The impact of pollutants on Scottish agriculture may be minor, except for tropospheric ozone, which may reduce some of the benefits of increased CO_2 concentrations and N deposition to plant growth. By contrast, increased UV-B radiation, resulting from depletion of stratospheric ozone is unlikely to have any direct effect on crop yield, as shown by field-based experiments which use realistic exposure levels.[16] Ironically, reduced sulphur emissions and deposition are 'harmful' in the sense that they are giving rise to sulphur deficiencies.

However, climate change is widely forecast to have a beneficial effect on the growth of Scottish forests, though not necessarily on their extent, unless there is a premium placed on carbon sequestration as part of a Government package to meet commitments under the Kyoto and subsequent protocols. The growth rate of *Picea sitchensis* in the uplands of Scotland is related more closely to mean annual temperature than to soil factors.[17] Alison, Proe and Matthews[18] found close positive correlations between the Yield Class of *P. sitchensis* in Scotland and temperatures in March, July, August and September, and negative correlations with winter temperatures. They concluded that an increase of 1C would raise Yield Classes by about 3 m^3 ha^{-1} a^{-1}. There is, in fact, good evidence that the Yield Class of upland conifer plantations has been increasing over the last 30–50 years by about 1 m^3 ha^{-1} a^{-1} per decade. Simulation models suggest that about half of this increase may be attributable to increasing atmospheric CO_2, N deposition and temperature and that, if this is so, substantial further increases in growth rate may occur during the 21st century.[12]

Impacts on natural flora and fauna

Climate change is likely to threaten some habitats and species in Scotland, and some plant communities may change, but overall the impacts are not predicted to be as severe or adverse as may be feared. In the absence of major droughts, warming at this latitude increases biodiversity. Hill *et al*(8) suggested that many, perhaps most, of the species in the UK Biodiversity Group's Priority List will either be little affected or respond to climate change positively. The flora and fauna in southern Scotland is likely to be enriched, but few lowland species are capable of invading the acid moorlands. Some species may spread to occupy areas which become favourable for them, but many will not: Collingham, Hill and Huntley[19] predicted that it might take 350–400 years for *Tilia europaea* (lime) to migrate unaided from northern England to the Scottish Borders. Thus, although subtle changes may occur within plant communities, individual species may spread and some reserve areas may need to be redesignated, it will be a long time before there are major landscape shifts altering the biogeographical zones defined by Carey *et al.*[20]

Also, the threat of alien plant species invading native habitats is thought to be slight, including the spread of *Acer pseudoplatanus* (sycamore) and *Rhododendron ponticum*.[21] The majority of species that could spread have been in Scotland for a long time in gardens and waste places or are already present in England or Wales. The sea is an effective barrier for most plants and animals and the flora and fauna of Britain is unlikely to change much in the next 100 years, despite climate change.[8]

However, there are some notable local impacts of climate change. First, it is inevitable that some Scottish alpine and subalpine habitats will be lost, bearing in mind that, in Scotland, a 1.8C rise in temperature is equivalent to 300 m in altitude. Many plant species (especially those currently restricted to north-facing slopes) which are adapted to low temperatures or tolerant of solifluction (soil movement caused by freeze-thaw cycles) will be out-competed by species invading from below and 'mountain' species such as the ptarmigan, dotterel and snow bunting will lose their habitats. Second, sea level rise will eventually lead to the loss of salt marsh and mudflats in low lying firths in Scotland, which support internationally significant numbers of overwintering ducks, geese and wading birds and are important staging areas during annual migrations.[8] Third, warmer sea, river and loch temperatures are likely to alter fish populations, notably affecting salmon and trout. Changes in sea currents have already been implicated as one possible reason for the recent fall in wild salmon numbers in Scotland, and any lowering in oxygen concentrations in river waters in response to warming will adversely affect salmon and trout and favour less valuable species such as pike.[13] Fourth, concern has been expressed over fragile mires in the Flow Country and similar areas where dubh lochains owe their existence to impeded drainage and may be unstable. The stratigraphy of Scottish blanket bogs shows that they have been very responsive to climate change in the past.[22] Fifth, there is the risk of climatic or impact surprises, which is always present, but will increase – especially the risk of severe floods, storms and outbreaks of insect pests. Pests of heather moorland, such as the magpie moth, or of exotic coniferous forests, such as the spruce aphid, could become a serious problem.

As mentioned, increased levels of tropospheric ozone may well become the most important air pollutant issue for vegetation of all kinds, if the high levels predicted by some modellers are realized. By contrast, levels of acidifying pollutants, other than N, are unlikely to remain damaging for soils and freshwaters in many parts of Scotland after 2010 as emission controls become effective.[11]

The effects of continued and maybe increasing N deposition are more problematic. Critical loads for ecosystems in Europe are set at 5–10 kg N ha^{-1} a^{-1} to cause declines in mosses and lichens in ombrotrophic bogs, 10–15 kg N ha^{-1} a^{-1} to reduce species diversity in montane grasslands and 15–20 kg N ha^{-1} a^{-1} for the transition from heather to grass and changes in the ground flora in acidic woodlands. It is difficult to find unequivocal evidence that N is driving these vegetation changes in Scotland, but there is reason to suspect that N deposition is at least partly responsible for the disappearance of bryophytes, including *Racomitrium* moss heath, in some upland areas, although increased grazing is considered to be a factor.[23] There is, however, clear evidence of species changes due to N enrichment downwind of livestock units, where N inputs are commonly 40–80 kg N ha^{-1} a^{-1} (Pitcairn pers comm.). By inference it may be concluded that continued N deposition in the range 10–30 kg N ha^{-1} a^{-1}, combined perhaps with increased N mineralization at warmer temperatures, could cause widespread changes in heather moorlands and high altitude heaths which cover so much of Scotland and have vegetation specifically adapted to nutrient poor conditions.

LAND-USE CHANGE

Agriculture

For the last century, at least rural land use in Scotland has been dominated by agriculture and currently contributed 2% of Scottish GDP (1% in the rest of UK) and a gross output of £1.9billion in 1998 (£2.5billion in 1995). Land cover and the structure of land holdings in Scotland today are the result of natural and human induced processes that have taken place predominantly over that time period. As elsewhere, the extent of agriculture in Scotland is determined by soil and climate. On this basis, only about 17%* of the land is suitable for arable agriculture whereas 38% is suitable for pasture based livestock systems, with a further 30–40% available for extensive grazing by sheep and cattle. Climate change may extend the area suited to arable cropping but probably by no more than 5%. Some 45–55% is suitable for productive forest trees and woodland. Currently, 73% (5.5mHa) of the land is in agriculture and because it is such a dominant land use, any change in agriculture is likely

---

* 17% of land suitable for intensive agriculture includes LCA classes 1.0–3.2. 38% of land suitable for sown grass and permanent pasture includes LCA classes 1.0–5.2 45–50% of land suitable for forestry includes LCA classes 1–5

to have a significant impact on other land uses and consequently on the economic, social and environmental structure of rural areas. In relation to the environment, it is important to note that at least 25% (over 2.0mHa) of the land is designated in one form or another for conservation purposes.*

Looking at historical trends, since 1944 the area of tillage in Scotland has declined and the proportion of different crops grown has changed as new crops and crop varieties have been introduced and bred, and as consumer demand has changed. Whereas in 1944 there was a need to produce as much of our primary food supply as possible, now, in a situation of low demand, a considerable area is set-aside. Much of the oversupply of primary food products has occurred in response to the incentives created by the EU Common Agricultural Policy. While reductions in the area of tillage has occurred, the level of physical outputs have been largely maintained or increased because of agriculture's considerable success in improving productivity over the period. Improved efficiency and intensification is also reflected in our pasture based livestock industries. Livestock numbers have been maintained, even though a significant amount of land has been lost to forestry and urban infrastructure. Furthermore, even though overall milk production has declined as the number of dairy cows have been reduced, the milk yield per cow has increased, thus partly compensating for the overall decline and again demonstrating the capacity of agriculture to continue to increase its productivity.

Despite all this, however, it is the underlying market trends and the potential to develop new markets, and their impact on the economic performance of primary food production that will determine agriculture's future. In a recent analysis,[24] it was concluded that changes in the policy structures that have surrounded agriculture for a long time are not the primary instruments that will determine future change in agriculture. Rather it is low growth in product demand and downward pressures on prices that will determine change. In Scotland, we can see this continuing decline in the outputs from both the livestock and crop sectors. Despite there being significant year to year variation, the mean decline in output from crops is estimated to have been £5.5m per annum in real terms since

---

* National Scenic Areas (1.0mHa), ESAs (1.5mHa), SSSIs (0.84mHa) but these areas overlap.

1973. The decline in livestock output in real terms over the same period has been much more consistent at £26.4m per annum. Arresting this decline will not be easy and, though it is reasonable to assume that both crop and livestock production will continue to be important industries in Scotland, there is considerable uncertainty about their ultimate size in the longer term.

As McInerney[24] points out, the crucially important fact for conventional agricultural production is that the income elasticity of demand for food in the UK is now only about 0.2. Thus, even if consumer's incomes in real terms rise by 1.5% per annum over the next 10 years, as they have in the '90s, expenditure on food will increase by only 3% which converts to a demand for primary products from agriculture of 2.5%. The message for the agricultural sector is that, if it does not adapt, its incomes will rise by 2–3% while everyone else's will go up by 15%. In order to retain the existing parity between the incomes of full-time farmers and those in the rest of the economy over the next 10 years, there would need to be an 11% reduction in the number of farmers which, as it turns out, is the same rate of reduction that has been taking place over the last 25 years within the UK. As we have observed there has also been a relentless increase in efficiency within the industry over the same period of around 2% per annum and there is every prospect that the available and developing technologies have the potential to maintain that level of improvement though much will depend on the public's perception and acceptance of these technologies.

The conclusion for the longer term, irrespective of the policy changes that may arise from WTO negotiations EU CAP reform, and EU Agenda 2000, is that agriculture will be characterised by a low but highly selective growth in demand for its primary produce, downward pressure on prices, and higher resource productivity. The consequences for land use change seem inevitable. There will be less land in conventional primary food production and there will be a change in the relative intensity that land is farmed, depending on farm size, farm type/farming system and land quality. For example, organic and integrated farming systems have emerged in recent years as more extensive and environmentally friendly approaches to farming. It is not obvious, however, as to the extent these systems will be more widely adopted but, being essentially low input: low output and labour intensive systems, they do offer an alternative way forward though their more extensive use of land would suggest the need for larger areas of land to achieve a farm income similar to that from conventional farming. But much will depend on product demand and price and funding support, for conversion. In the UK the area converting or converted to organic farming has increased from 50,000ha in 1995 to almost 300,000ha in 1999. The evidence from elsewhere in Europe is that organic farming has expanded most rapidly where it has received high levels of funding support, e.g. Austria, Finland, Germany and Italy. The provision of additional support for conversion to organic farming may have a similar effect in Scotland. Whether it will be long lasting remains to be seen.

But the question arises that if less land is required for primary food production how will the potential surplus be used apart from being used more extensively. In recent times, certainly since the Second World War, and particularly in hill and upland areas, when there has been an economic downturn in agriculture, forestry has taken up the land released from agriculture. How likely is this over the next five decades?

Forestry

When the Forestry Commission was established in 1919 to create a strategic reserve of timber for three years the forest area in Scotland stood at 4.5% of the land area. Since then the woodland area has expanded steadily and in 1995 covered some 19% of the Scottish land area of the Scottish land area and is estimated to contribute around £800m per year to the Scottish economy exclusive of the contribution derived from its non-market benefits.

After the Second World War it became apparent that the policy objective of maintaining a standing reserve of timber for use during a period of war became irrelevant. The rationale for afforestation came to be based on commercial and social objectives. However, in the late 1980s the grants and tax concessions that had encouraged widespread coniferous afforestation of land released from agriculture were removed. Moreover, following the rapid expansion of upland forests in the 1960s and 1970s, the amendment of the Wildlife and Countryside Act in 1985 required a 'reasonable balance' to be struck between timber production and natural heritage considerations. Since then, grant schemes have been introduced that encourage the planting of broadleaved woodlands on better quality land on farms and also are designed to encourage the regeneration of native woodlands. The changes that have taken place in the area and proportion of different forest types in Scotland demonstrates that an increasing proportion of new planting is broadleaved woodland (currently 60%). These changes represent an ascendancy of the conservation and recreational benefits of forestry and a relative decline in the weight placed on traditional or commercial objectives of forestry policy.

Recently, however, David Bills, at the end of his first four year term as the Director-General of the Forestry Commission expressed his concern about how current market conditions might influence how policy-makers continue to view a multiple function approach to forestry development.[25] This is because there has been a fall in log prices of almost 50% since 1996. Indeed, coniferous standing sales prices in Great Britain were 29% lower in the year to September 1999, compared to the previous year. Despite this decline and gloomy market forecasts, both new planting and restocking have remained at the level of the previous year. Supply and demand for timber also remained reasonably constant over the same period.

However, even though the UK is self-sufficient for only about 20% of its wood products and it is predicted that there will be a shortfall in meeting the demand for softwood by 2050 it remains uncertain, under present market conditions and international cost-competitiveness, (eg costs of transporting timber) as to whether there is sufficient commercial incentive to invest in extensive new planting. For the near future, unless there are dramatic changes in timber prices or a significant fall in land prices or new markets for forest products are found, widespread conversion of agricultural land to forestry seems unlikely. However, other considerations will influence new planting in Scotland. These will emerge as part of the implementation of the Rural Development Regulation and Agenda 2000. New planting will continue to be encouraged through the Woodland Grant Scheme and the Farm Woodland Premium Scheme. Both schemes, along with the Woodland Improvement Grants and Annual Management Grants, are designed to bring about a further integration of forestry and agriculture, increase recreational access and encourage the regeneration of native species. There is also the prospect that a significant role for forestry linked to international carbon sequestration and carbon-trading strategies could be established. It is reasonable to predict under these circumstances, therefore, that at the very least, there will be a continued but modest increase in the area of forest in Scotland and that it will have a high natural heritage value.

So what does this analysis of the future for agriculture and forestry imply for our natural heritage and for environmental protection?

NATURAL HERITAGE AND ENVIRONMENTAL PROTECTION

Since 1970, and particularly since the introduction of the Wildlife and Countryside Act (1983) there has been a genuine concern about the impact of the rural land use industries on the rural environment as well as the impact of anthropogenic pollution arising from urban-based industrial and power generating activities. The creation of the Environmental Protection Agencies is a direct outcome of these concerns. Whatever the mechanisms used, we can expect environmental protection to become progressively more stringent over the next 50 years and particularly so with respect to the use of the land resource and its impact on river catchment management. But reversing these trends is no longer just associated with a reaction to the extreme exploitation of land for production purposes. Countryside agencies, such as Scottish Natural Heritage, and non-government voluntary bodies focus increasingly on environmental enhancement and proactive environmental management. This is because there is also a more explicit demand from the public for environmental goods and services associated with recreation, sport, tourism and a general enjoyment of the countryside.

So finding ways whereby our land can be shared more equitably and responsibly is important for the future. It is not only important with respect to the wider social and cultural benefits that can be achieved but also because of the additional economic benefits that can be brought to our rural areas. The legislation related to feudal tenure, community ownership, access and the establishment of national parks will all have an important bearing on how the land can be used to benefit the environment and people of Scotland as a whole.

In this context, for example, tourism in Scotland, though affected significantly by the value of the pound, has become a significant component of economic activity and rural policy development. The Scottish Tourist Board estimates that of the 11.2 million trips taken in Scotland in 1996, around 6.4 million trips can be regarded as being associated with rural tourism.[26] These trips are estimated to represent £692m or 46% of the total expenditure on tourism in Scotland.* Nor can we ignore the potential for developing complementary activities based on the use of the countryside. For example, the contribution that is made from field sports can complement agriculture and create a greater potential for recreational sport and tourism in rural areas. It has been estimated that 60,000 direct and 30,000 indirect jobs are associated with field sports in the UK, involved with game valued at £12–18m, venison at £9m and fish at £650k†.[27] Are there further opportunities of extending this type of complementary use of our countryside that provides access and a country side experience as well as income to the farm or estate?

Access and the increasing numbers of people that will visit and retire to the countryside, however, will inevitably bring pressures on the physical resource of rural areas. Social behaviour and attitudes towards the countryside, and the dynamic of urban and rural cultures over this period, will inevitably create a multitude and potentially conflicting set of demands upon the countryside. Recreational, sporting and tourist demands have the potential, on the one hand, to diversify the rural economy but, on the other hand, to create pressures on the physical resource that may be environmentally unsustainable. Equally, policies that are designed to create inward investment and diversity of employment within rural communities have the potential to facilitate structural change in land use and create stability in rural populations and service provision, but they could also bring about fundamental change in the value of natural capital and in the culture of our rural areas. Managing increasing numbers of people visiting our countryside is likely to become a primary concern for the successful management of the natural heritage over the next 50 years. The future designation of land for conservation and protection purposes will need to take this into account, while at the same time creating opportunities for access. This will not be a trivial task.

---

* But much of this tourism depends on ready access to the countryside. It will be important therefore to develop agri-environment and countryside schemes whereby land managers deliver environmental goods and improve access. Where now they receive support linked to food production these incentives or payments need to be linked to more positive land management for wildlife and habitats, the planting of trees, and the creation of attractive landscape features and visual amenity

† There are at least 25,000 associated businesses with a turnover of £1b. In Scotland, for example, it has been estimated that 1000 FTE jobs are directly involved in deer management, 520 FTE with River Tweed fishing and over 500 FTE jobs on Scottish grouse moors

IMPLICATIONS FOR THE ENVIRONMENT AND LAND USE OF THE FUTURE

What do these changes in climate and the agriculture and forestry industries and the requirements for more sensitive environmental management and countryside access mean for the environment and land use of the future in Scotland?

As far as agriculture in Scotland is concerned, large farms (100–<200 ESUs*) with land of good quality are increasingly likely to become intensive agri-businesses with the aim of achieving greater efficiency in production through optimising inputs and maximising the usable product to meet precise requirements. They are also likely to get bigger. These farms are also likely to benefit most from climate change since they will tend to be on the better soils in the east of the country. There will certainly be the potential to grow a greater range of crops on these farms in the future.[28]

Medium-sized businesses (40–<100 ESUs) are on the one hand likely to pursue a conventional route of enlargement and continue as before within an ever tighter economic environment, their continuing viability depending on availability of capital and innovative management. Climate change may provide scope for growing a greater proportion of arable crops on these farms as a consequence of higher temperatures and extended growing season. But some will inevitably fail and the land released will go towards the enlargement of similar sized successful businesses. On the other hand, many of these medium-sized businesses may become increasingly diversified reflecting a new attitude of entrepreneurship that is already developing among some farmers, seeking both to add value to primary produce and to exploit environmental goods on the farm. Smaller businesses (8–<40 ESUs) are increasingly likely to operate on a part-time basis or be sold to hobby farmers who are not dependent upon their source of income from farming.

That land will convert to other forms of use is certain, if farm and estate businesses are to remain viable.[29] Though present market conditions and fiscal arrangements suggest that forestry expansion will be slight, circumstances may change. It does seem reasonable, bearing in mind the recent

---

* 1 European Size Unit (ESU) is approximately equivalent to £1000 of farm Standard Gross Margin (SGM). The total SGM for a farm is calculated by multiplying its crop areas and livestock numbers by the appropriate SGM and then summing the result for all enterprises on the farm.

history of forestry development, to assume that over the next 50 years there will be a modest increase in the area of tree cover within the context of a multiple purpose forest and woodland strategy. But equally, it is likely that some land, particularly of marginal fertility and remoteness, may be used neither for agriculture or forestry. Some land is likely to be taken in hand and managed for conservation purposes by voluntary bodies. And, it seems inevitable that some land may be subject to no management whatsoever, which will have implications for nature conservation management and objectives. Restructuring of land holdings within this general context seems inevitable.

Such developments, of course, are likely to take different routes in different parts of Scotland in relation to the implementation of EU Agenda 2000, and the EU Rural Development Regulation.* This regulation encourages the integration of agriculture within the broader context of rural development and increasing the proportion of structural funds, at the expense of commodity support, should provide opportunities for the development of a range of farm and land based activities over many areas of Scotland. Such possibilities are likely to include farm woodland, native woodland regeneration, industrial biomass crops for local heat and electricity production, nature conservation management, sport and recreation, tourism and accommodation provision. The Regulation will also specifically focus on support for sustainable farming in Scotland's Less Favoured Areas (LFAs).

In some areas with a high potential for efficient and demand led agriculture, strategic regional planning and resource allocation might be

* Rural Development Directive
  – The creation of a stronger, more competitive agriculture and forestry (investment aid to agricultural holdings, processing and marketing of quality products, agricultural training, aid to young farmers, and early retirement schemes for farmers over 55, and less favoured payments on an acreage rather than on a headage basis).
  – Creating a living countryside, through the pursuit of increased competitiveness and an improved quality of life (farm and off-farm diversification to promote pluriactivity and pluri income sources, small infrastructure measures, renovation of villages, promotion of tourism and crafts, and basic services for the rural economy and population).
  – Maintaining the environment and preserving Europe's unique rural heritage (protection of the environment, conservation of the rural cultural heritage, and animal welfare measures)

organised accordingly. In other areas, the same argument may be appropriate for forestry. In yet other areas, which may be far the greater proportion of our land in Scotland, a more appropriate route may be to encourage an integration of agriculture and woodland/forestry with a region's recreation and tourist potential. There may also be areas where it is judged that any intervention would be counterproductive and that it would be more appropriate for nature to take its course. Such an area by area approach would allow a closer examination of the balance that needs to be struck between achieving economic, social and environmental objectives on a local basis, within a set of policies that have sustainable development at their core.

CONCLUSION

Understanding the trade-off between the potential benefits and the complex outcomes that can arise from policy and decision making at all levels will be crucial to managing our future: it is what sustainable development is about. It provides the conceptual framework within which future land use, the management of climate change and the environment, restructuring and rural development can take place. Climate change is likely to bring with it more positive than negative effects, though loss of some local habitats seems inevitable. That primary food production will be a less dominant feature of land use in some areas of Scotland seems certain. Restructuring of land holdings and changes in land ownership are also inevitable. The real question is whether we choose to allow the full force of the market to determine its rate and extent, or whether there is an argument for intervention. That a greater proportion of our land is likely to become available and required for public access and recreational use seems also certain. Whether we have or will have the policies and measures in place to manage such change is a matter for continuing debate and action.

Ultimately, it is the balance that Scottish society chooses between achieving its economic, social equity and environmental goals that will determine the environment and land use of the future. It will depend also on how clever we become in achieving wealth creation and economic competitiveness, while at the same time conserving, protecting and enhancing our natural heritage, and importantly, whether we are prepared to make the necessary investment to do so. There are no easy answers but this is the challenge that we, in Scotland, have to face. If devolution means anything, it is that with our inherent potential to solve problems together, we have been given the opportunity to do so.

REFERENCES

1. K B Matthews, S M Craw, S Elder, A R Sibbald and I MacKenzie, 'Applying Genetic Algorithms to Multi-objective Land Use Planning'. In *Proceedings of Genetic and Evolutionary Computation Conference* (GECCO 2000; in press), (2000).
2. A N R Law, R V Birnie and A R Sibbald, 'New Developments in Forecasting Land Use Change'. MLURI Annual Report 1999. J G Polhill, N M Gotts and A N R Law, 'Initiative versus Non-Imitative Strategies in a Land Use Simulation'. Cybernetics and Systems (2000).
3. C Langton, R Bunkhart, M Daniels and A Lancaster, 'The Swarm Simulation System'. WWW pages: http://www.swarm.org. (2000).
4. D Pearce, 'Blueprint – Measuring Sustainable Development'. Earthscan Publications, London, 1996.
5. M E Mann, R S Bradley, M K Hughes, 'Northern hemisphere temperatures during the past millennium: inferences, uncertainties and limitations,' *Geophysical Research Letters* **26**, (1999), 759–762.
6. Inter-governmental Panel on Climate Change, *Climate Change 1995: The Science of Climate Change*. Cambridge, 1996.
7. M Hulme, G J Jenkins, *Climate change scenarios for the UK: scientific report*. UK Climate Impacts Programme Technical Report No. 2, Climatic Research Unit, Norwich (1998), 80pp.
8. M O Hill, T E Downing, P M Berry, B J Coppins, P S Hammond, M Marquiss, D B Roy, M G Telfer, D Welch, 'Climate changes and Scotland's natural heritage'. *Scottish Natural Heritage*, Report 32 (1999), Edinburgh.
9. PORG. *Ozone in the United Kingdom*. Photochemical Oxidants Review Group. UK Department of Environment, Transport and Regions. 234pp (1997).
10. D Fowler, J N Cape, M Coyle, C Flechard, J Kuylenstierna, K Hicks, D Derwent, C Johnson, D Stevenson, 'The global exposure of forests to air pollutants', *Water, Air and Soil Pollution* 116 (1999), 5–32.
11. CLAG. *Critical levels of air pollutants for the United Kingdom*. Report of the Critical Loads Advisory Group, Department of the Environment, London (1996).
12. M G R Cannell, D Fowler, C E R Pitcairn, 'Climate change and pollutant impacts on Scottish vegetation', *Botanical Journal of Scotland* 49 (1998), 301–313. M G R Cannell, J H M Thornley, D C Mobbs, A D Friend, 'UK conifer forests may be growing faster in response to increased N deposition, atmospheric CO_2 and temperature', *Forestry* 71 (1998), 277–296.
13. A Kerr, S Shackley, R Milne, S Allen, *Climate change: Scottish implications scoping study*. Scottish Executive, Central Research Unit, Edinburgh (1999).
14. A C Armstrong, D J Parsons, J R Turnpenny, A M Matthews, K C Cooper and J A Clark, 'Integrated models of livestock systems for climate change studies. 1.

Grazing systems'. *Global Change Biology,* In press. R A C Mitchell, D W Lawlor, V J Mitchell, C L Gibbad, E M White, J R Porter, 'Effects of elevated CO2 concentration and increased temperature on winter wheat: test of ARCWHEAT1 model'. *Plant, Cell and Environment* 18 (1995), 736–748. M Parry, I Carson, T Rehman, R Tranter, P Jones, D Mortimer, M Livermore, J Little, *Economic implications of climate change on agriculture in England and Wales.* Report 1. Jackson Environment Institute, University of East Anglia (1999). J H M Thornley, M G R Cannell, 'Temperate grassland responses to climate change: an analysis using the Hurley Pasture Model', *Annals of Botany* 80 (1997), 205–221.

15. A Davies, T Jenkins, A Pike, J Shao, I Carson, C J Pollock, M L Parry, 'Modelling the predicted geographic and economic response of UK cropping systems to climate change scenarios: the case of potatoes', *Annal of Applied Biology* 130 (1997), 167–178.

16. J Stephen, R Woodfin, J E Corlett, N D Paul, H G Jones, P G Ayres, 'Response of barley and pea crops to supplementary UV-B radiation', *Journal of Agricultural Science* 132 (1998), 253–261.

17. R Worrell, D C Malcolm. 'Productivity of Sitka spruce in northern Britain. II. Prediction from site factors', *Forestry* 63 (1990), 119–128.

18. S M Alison, M F Proe, K B Matthews, 'The production and distribution of general yield classes of Sitka spruce in Scotland by empirical analysis of site factors using a geographic information system'. *Canadian Journal of Forest Research* 24, 2166–2177.

19. Y C Collingham, M O Hill, B Huntley, 'The migration of sessile organisms: a simulation model with measurable parameters' *Journal of Vegetation Science* 7 (1996), 831–846.

20. P D Carey, C D Preston, M O Hill, M B Usher, S M Wright, 'An environmentally defined biogeographical zonation of Scotland designed to reflect species distributions', *Journal of Ecology* 83 (1995), 833–845.

21. M O Hill, S M Wright, J C Dring, L G Firbank, S J Manchester, J M Croft, 'The potential for spread of alien species in England following climatic change, English Nature, Research *Report* No. 90 (1994), EN, Peterborough.

22. K E Barber, R W Baterbee, S J Brooks and 18 others,.' Proxy records of climate change in the UK over the last two millennia: documentary change and sedimentary records from lakes and bogs' *Journal of the Geological Society* 156 (1996), 369–380.

23. J A Badeley, D B A Thompson, J A Lee, 'Regional and historical variation in the nitrogen content of *Racomitrium lanuginosum* in Britain in relation to atmospheric nitrogen deposition', *Environmental Pollution* 84 (1994), 189–196. C E R Pitcairn, D Fowler, J Grace, 'Deposition of fixed atmospheric nitrogen and foliar nitrogen content of bryophytes and *Calluna vulgaris* (L.) Hull', *Environmental Pollution* 88, 193–205.

24. J McInerney, 'Agriculture at the Crossroads', *Journal of the Royal Agricultural Society of England,* 160, 8 (1999).

25. D Bills, 'Looking Back', *Scottish Forestry,* 53(4), 210 (1999).

26. Scottish Tourist Board, 'British Tourism in Scotland 1996 – Environmental Location. Scottish Tourist Board, Edinburgh (1998).

27. M S Hankey, 'The Role of Field Sports', Heather Trust Conference, Battleby 1999.

28. M Shucksmith and V Herrman, Attitudes of Behaviour of Farmers in the Grampian Uplands (1999). T J Maxwell, 'Rural Land Use Research – Creating Sustainable Solutions for Our Land and People, MLURI Annual Report 1998, page 6.

Part Two. The Drivers of Change

3

The Economy

J A Peat

INTRODUCTION

THIS CONFERENCE WAS held at a fascinating time so far as policies for the Scottish economy are concerned. Work is underway, essentially within the Scottish Executive and led by Henry McLeish, on 'A Framework for Scottish Economic Policy'. I am an advocate of the development, especially in the context of a devolved legislature alongside devolved administration, of the development of economic policies 'made in Scotland to suit Scotland'. This pending Framework document is crucial as the first genuine opening salvo in the moves by Executive and Parliament in that direction.

We need a full, frank and transparent debate on the Scottish economy and Scottish economic policies. With this in mind my colleague Stephen Boyle and I co-wrote last year *'An Illustrated Guide to the Scottish Economy'*,[1] which I commend to all those wishing an introductory overview to our economy. Further, on 27th March the Scottish Council Foundation published *'Towards an Economic Policy for Scotland'*.[2] This is the first output of the Economic Policy Network of the Foundation. I chair that Network and co-wrote their first report with Graham Leicester, the Foundation's Director. A number of issues touched upon in this paper are dealt with at greater length in the Foundation report.

In developing a set of economic policies for Scotland the Executive will need to take account of a range of issues addressed by this conference – by no means only those covered in the economists' papers.

OBJECTIVES FOR THE ECONOMY

In broad terms economists should not set the objectives for economic policy in Scotland – or elsewhere. Broad objectives should be set by the

Scottish people, or by their representatives. Then it is for economists to advise how these objectives can best be met. In the course of this process economists can aid society and Parliament. They can help to determine the extent to which differing objectives are mutually consistent and how adverse trade-offs can best be minimised. Also economists as individuals and members of society have as much right as any other individual to have views on overall objectives.

Two general statements on economic objectives for Scotland are set out below. These are statements by Scottish Enterprise and the Minister for Enterprise and Lifelong learning respectively.

> We exist to promote economically, environmentally and socially-sustainable development in Scotland . . . (resulting) . . . in more jobs, greater prosperity and a higher quality of life for all. *(Scottish Enterprise)*

> Our priorities as set out in *Making it Work Together – A Programme for Government* include creating a culture of enterprise; providing training for skills that match jobs for the future; widening access to further and higher education; and creating a culture of lifelong learning, increasing adult participation in education and training. To help build a successful and prosperous Scotland, we are also committed to tackling poverty and to supporting sustainable development. *(Henry McLeish MSP)*

I find it easier to break objectives for the economy into three categories – efficiency, equity and externalities. In my view, this delineation helps us to determine, more precisely for policy purposes, relative priority for different components of what we can term the economic objective function.

Efficiency

Used here in the macro or over-arching sense, 'efficiency' can be taken to encapsulate pure output maximisation. One possible goal for the economy, for example, might be to maximise output growth such that average output per head is as high as feasible. In this context, output would probably be better measured not by GDP but by GNP – Gross National Product – as this assesses the income retained within Scotland. It would also be necessary to place this objective in at least a medium term context, as a dash for 'excessive' growth in the short term will in practice reduce the rate of growth achieved in that medium term.

Equity

It is also perfectly feasible that maximising total national 'output' alone should not be the be all and end all of policy. Given the statement quoted above, that is clearly the Scottish Executive's view. It is perfectly legitimate for economic policy to embrace other objectives too. For example, there will be social or other 'equity' factors to take into account. It might be determined that, at least to some extent, enhanced social inclusion and/or a more equitable distribution of income or wealth would be an acceptable trade off against increase in GNP. The preferred re-distribution could be between income groups, geographical areas, urban/rural, or whatever.

Externalities

This term effectively encapsulates all other wider or 'spin-off' effects of policy, whether intended or otherwise. For example, in addition to concerns about the distribution of output, there are difficulties with the market price basis upon which we measure national wealth. GDP is a measure of the good, the bad and the ugly in that it records all money transactions, regardless of the purpose of the transaction. So long as money changes hands, GDP measures growth in crime, traffic congestion, the cost of cleaning up the environment, the cost of treating an unhealthy population, and many more negative factors. It is clear that the simple objective of growth in GDP is insufficient to inform policy, given the numerous ways in which GDP can grow even as society deteriorates.

AN ECONOMIC PEN PICTURE

In brief summary, Scotland is an open economy, subject to intense and inevitably increasing competition across a range of sectors and activities. The key trading links are first with the rest of the UK and then with the rest of Europe. Even when trading with these closer neighbours remoteness and high transport costs are issues, simply adding to the importance of continuing to strive to be competitive and increasing productivity and value added.

The degree of competition can only increase. This will happen as world trade generally becomes more open; or perhaps as trade within (say) three great trading blocs becomes wholly open. Competition will increase as more economies progress and emerge as efficient competitors to Scotland

and the rest of the UK. Competition will also tend to increase as barriers to entry in different economic sectors – services as well as manufacturing – break down and the transparency and availability of price and other information is accentuated.

This is, to me, the main initial impact of the e-commerce revolution, with the consequences that prices are constrained, margins squeezed and competition tightened yet further.

More detailed material is given in 'An Illustrated Guide'[1] for the key components and in the Royal Bank of Scotland's Economics Office 'Update Scotland' reports, as published on our website (www.rbs.co.uk/news/commentary).

MACRO EFFICIENCY VERSUS MICRO EFFICIENCY

I introduced above the concept of macro efficiency in the economy. Taking macro efficiency as the economic objective implies targeting economic growth alone, without any priority to equity or externality issues. Pure macro efficiency is highly unlikely to be selected as Scotland's over-arching goal. However, whatever set of objectives are selected, it will be essential, for the competitiveness reasons summarised above, that we are 'efficient' in micro-economic terms.

Endogenous growth theory – as famously espoused by Gordon Brown and his Economic Adviser Ed Balls – is all about how economies can become more micro efficient by improvements on the supply side of the economy. The gist of the argument is that macro economic policies (primarily monetary and fiscal policies) should be aimed at creating and maintaining a stable, low inflation and a low interest rate environment for all agents within the economy. The intention should be to keep growth as close as possible to the sustainable trend, the maximum rate feasible for the duration without inflation accelerating and cyclical problems emerging.

The work on the supply side should aim at increasing micro efficiency. By making the economy operate more flexibly and efficiently, with less under-utilised or misused resources, the sustainable growth rate can increase. Bringing more inputs into play and achieving more output per unit of input will enable the economy to grow faster for longer without inflation risks increasing. That in turn permits more scope to achieve whatever set of objectives are selected for the economic objective function.

UK economic policy is increasingly focused on the supply side. The key issues for Gordon Brown are, first, how participation rates in the economy can be increased and 'exclusion' reduced; and, second, how productivity and hence output per head can be raised. The types of factors that are involved in this context include: –

- Investment and innovation
- R&D
- Human capital
- Adaptability
- Competitiveness and 'contestability' of markets
- Entrepreneurial drive
- New firm formation and flux
- Institutional arrangements
- Infrastructure.

One good piece of news is that the evidence available suggests that, where the drive to higher output is via supply side policies, then there is less cause for concern about adverse trade-offs with the other objectives described earlier than is the case with the stringent macro management policies so often recommended by the International Monetary Fund (IMF).

The bad news is that there are a number of topics on this list for which Scottish performance is less satisfactory than we would wish. That applies to investment and to R&D (especially for Scottish owned companies): it applies to business start-ups – more in the central belt than elsewhere. Even with regard to human capital, we have a long way to go to match many of our peer group.

Whatever happens on objectives, we need more and more emphasis in Scotland on efficiency in the micro sense and more emphasis on competition and enhancing productivity. Some policies can be debated to help achieve these ends. Equally important, is that other policies which tend to reduce efficiency and competitiveness should be resisted. Policies aimed at achieving other perfectly respectable objectives should, wherever feasible, avoid adverse impacts on micro efficiency. It is welcome indeed that the powers of the Scottish Parliament include a wide range of topics of direct or indirect relevance to micro efficiency.

SCOTTISH ECONOMIC GOVERNANCE

Economic governance has changed in Scotland with the advent of the Parliament. It may change further as revisions are made to the Enterprise Network and other aspects of strategy formulation and policy delivery in Scotland, e.g. the role of the STB, local authorities, etc.

But there are also major changes in governance for the EU and the UK. In the UK we now have an independent Monetary Policy Committee (MPC) at the Bank of England, charged with running monetary policy in such a way as to meet an inflation target set out by the Chancellor of the Exchequer. Also clear rules have been laid down for the operation of fiscal policy, again limiting the role and flexibility of the Chancellor and the Treasury. In addition, Regional Development Agencies have been set up in England, with roles much more limited than SE or the WDA, but likely to grow rapidly. Then there is the move to elected mayors, and the debate about regional assemblies. Certainly economic governance is very much different from the time when I served briefly in HM Treasury in the mid 1980s.

I have referred briefly above to the role of the Scottish Parliament on the micro economic front. Its direct role on the macro side is highly limited. However, that does not mean that the Parliament does not have a wholly legitimate interest in macro policies. That interest should be recognised in the context of the evolving UK economic governance. For example, the Scottish Parliament may wish to express views on specific Budget priorities or on issues related to the UK's stance on EMU and the euro.

More specifically, the MPC is setting interest rates for the whole of the UK, including Scotland, and is charged with doing so in a way that takes account of variations in economic conditions and interests by region and sector. The Scottish Parliament has a clear interest in that policy. Should the Parliament, or more plausibly a Committee of the Parliament, have the right to question periodically the Governor of the Bank of England and members of the MPC about their work on monetary policy, in a Scottish economic context?

MEASUREMENT ISSUES

The key point under this heading is that Gross Domestic Product, as presently measured, is not a full and/or adequate measure of economic welfare in Scotland. In 'An Illustrated Guide' Stephen Boyle and I lay emphasis on the priority to enhancing data and research on our economy. I welcome the move to quarterly GDP data only a few months after the event – not by any means as rapidly as for the UK as a whole but a marked improvement. Further improvements are scheduled and I fully acknowledge both the commitment to improving data and the difficulty given the resource costs involved.

But I can still wish for more, as undoubtedly do my former colleagues in the Scottish Executive economics and statistics team. The Executive is committed to working on Gross *National* Product data. These allow for transfers in and out of the economy and thus provide a better measure of economic wealth retained in Scotland.

In addition to the GDP/GNP point, a major debate continues on valuation. In effect, the national accounts value everything that is priced, at the price that applies, but exclude everything that is not priced. Such items are implicitly deemed as of no value. Fighting crime and ill health, therefore, adds to national economic welfare as measured in the national accounts, while voluntary work does not.

Various pieces of work are underway to derive alternative national accounts. One classic example is of green national accounts. In these, environmental services are added to GDP or GNP, while environmental damage and defensive expenditures are subtracted.

While on the topic of valuation, it is worth under-scoring the point that market prices do not always reflect economic values. There can be distortions and these require adjustment before policies aimed at optimisation can sensibly be introduced. There are huge issues surrounding measurement of economic values and determining market based instruments to drive policy towards optimisation on the basis of corrected 'economic' prices.

One final point is that in many instances pragmatism does make sense. Seeking out the best in terms of economic measurement can often be the enemy of the good. Simple, but wholly clear, statements of what it is that policies are setting out to achieve and how that achievement can be measured will permit monitoring and evaluation that adds value to future decision making and policy formulation.

SOME CONCLUSIONS

We should be attempting to achieve a better understanding and agreement on objectives – which, in short-term,will involve the achievement of healthy growth that takes equity and externality trade offs into account. As an economist, I would prefer, in theory, a rigorous and quantified objective function of 'national economic welfare' which permits trade offs to be assessed consistently and objectively. As a realist, I accept that that is not what we shall get, but trust that we will move in the direction of clarity. We should focus on micro efficiency in all sectors and components of the economy, whatever our set of objectives. In setting policies that seek to ensure minimisation of adverse externalities it is desirable to estimate true economic costs and benefits, rather than relying on (possibly distorted) market prices. Further, it is almost always preferable, in theory and practice, to work to optimise with the grain of the market. In determining 'success' we will require both an improved articulation of what that means and enhanced measures of all the key components. Now is absolutely the right time for the debate to begin. We have the scope for independent policies in a range of areas, and the scope to influence policies at the UK level. GDP maximisation is not the be all and end all; but nebulous statements of other objectives will not assist the policy formation process. We need to be clear at all times.

As an economist with a micro bent, I shall continue to press the case for micro efficiency in Scotland and moving up the quality and productivity chain in all areas and sectors – and that means that both endogenous growth policy and the focus on the supply side make sense.

REFERENCES

1. J Peat and S Boyle, *An Illustrated Guide to the Scottish Economy*, Duckworth, London 1999.
2. Scottish Council Foundation, *Towards an Economic Policy for Scotland*, Scottish Council Foundation, Edinburgh, 2000.

4

Attitudes to Nature and the Ethics of Conservation

John M Francis

INTRODUCTION

My qualifications for writing on ethics are not as a Professor of Moral and Social Theology, but as a second generation nuclear scientist who, more than 30 years ago, was led astray into the fields of Theology and Ethics. I was appointed to direct a forward-looking project, based in Edinburgh, on 'Society, Religion & Technology' for the Church of Scotland. The SRT Project, as it is widely known, has gone from strength to strength over the intervening years. In 1998 a group consisting of professional scientists, ethicists and other scholars, working under the auspices of the Project, produced a very far-sighted and well-reviewed book on the ethics of genetic engineering in non-human species under the title 'Engineering Genesis'.[1] My own time as Director of the Project in the years 1970 to 1974 took me down some surprising paths which helped to inform and create an understanding of the 'attitudes to Nature' which prevail in Scotland and elsewhere.

I have structured the paper as follows Firstly, an element of personal narrative which goes back to 1972 and the first United Nations Conference on the Human Environment held in Stockholm. Secondly, I take another backward glance at the origins of what we all now recognise in the Western industrialised world as our historic attempt to continue to dominate or subdue Nature, namely, the theological roots of the so-called ecological crisis. Thirdly, I shall take a brief look at the principles and ethics of conservation as reflected in our present statutory framework in Britain. And finally, a slightly more altruistic reflection on what we ought to be doing about the statutory framework for conservation in Scotland and elsewhere.

UN CONFERENCE ON THE HUMAN ENVIRONMENT   1972

In June 1972 I was privileged to be part of the international Non-Government Organisation (NGO) group invited to attend the UN Conference on the Human Environment in Stockholm. On this occasion, I was part of the turbulence on the streets outside the main conference centre where the environmental protest movement was cutting its teeth alongside a range of citizens' groups which had arrived from all over the world. The Swedish Government in the person of Prime Minister Olaf Palme did not overreact to this growing presence on the streets and most of the lively and colourful demonstrations went off calmly enough and with reasonably good humour. But as the days passed, there was evidence of a significant and growing tension between the drafting committees, made up largely of Government officials from the UN member states working on the details of the Conference Declarations in the main conference chambers, and the large environmental lobby hidden away from the central hub of the conference in one of the Stockholm suburbs.

This Environmental Forum arranged by the NGO group had a formidable line-up which included people of the stature of Margaret Mead, Paul Ehrlich and Barry Commoner contingent. Consequently, while the debate was cogent, intense and very urgent, the emerging message was also becoming crystal clear. Unless the industrialised nations were collectively prepared to adopt a different attitude to Nature and to protection of the natural environment, then everyone, including the developing nations, would be heading for serious trouble and potential longer term ecological risks.

The debate addressed many issues. In many of the developing nations the increasing problems of sustaining adequate freshwater supplies led to the need to reduce the biological and chemical contamination of ground water in many parts of the world. Trans-boundary air pollution, particularly amongst the European nations, was generating acid rain with many consequential effects in forests and rivers. Increasing mineral extraction rates were raising questions about non-renewable resources. Measures to prevent ocean dumping of toxic chemicals and other waste materials were called for. And, inevitably, there were signs of increasing awareness and concerns about the general overloading of limits to the carrying capacity of natural systems. The arguments and the statistics in support of the need for a major shift in our attitude to Nature were overwhelming. As the week of inter-Governmental meetings drew to a close, the voices out there on the fringe became increasingly demanding and strident. They had a serious point to make and it seemed not to be registering with sufficient clarity in the official discussions.

I was fortunate also to have full press accreditation and so was able to move between the two opposing camps, including attendance at the press briefings given by the various Heads of State, Government Ministers and UN agency directors. At the same time I had the opportunity to share my observations with some very experienced journalists who were covering the event – including John Maddox from Nature, Anthony Tucker for The Guardian and Gerald Leach from The Observer.

The consensus amongst this group was that they could detect a real sense of a transition – attitudes to Nature were beginning to change – and two symbolic facts had confirmed this for them. The first of these was the image of the planet and the vulnerable layer of the biosphere when photographed for the first time from the Apollo spacecraft. This image provided the backdrop in the main conference chamber one evening for the launch of the book – 'Only One Earth' – by Barbara Ward and Rene Dubos.[2] The journalists were therefore ready to be persuaded that change might be possible, even among politicians and the general public, from an attitude which was almost totally exploitative towards Nature and natural resources to one that was better prepared to accept the boundaries of spaceship earth in Kenneth Boulding's famous phrase. They agreed that this new attitude might, just might, begin to take hold. Perhaps they were being unduly optimistic or had simply gone native during the period of the conference.[3] Anyway something was happening both in the conference chamber and on the street outside.

The second symbol was the crusade on the streets of Stockholm, led by various national and international protest groups to 'Save the Whale' – and as noted in Peter Stones book *Did We Save the Earth at Stockholm?*[3] – 'Inside the Old Riksdag the fate of the whales had become a symbol of the success or failure of the Conference.'

Subsequently this cause has been taken up around the globe and with some degree of success. The idea of single species conservation has begun to take hold in many countries but the question remains – 'Have general attitudes to nature, particularly in a country like Scotland, changed significantly over the past 25 years or so?' I suspect that the jury is still taking time to consider the implications of their verdict!

THE HISTORICAL PERSPECTIVE

I need to go back at this point to the extraordinary book by John Black – 'The Dominion of Man: the Search for Ecological Responsibility'[4] first published in 1970. At the time John Black was Professor of Forestry & Natural Resources in the University of Edinburgh, but he had based his book on a series of three Special University Lectures which he gave at the invitation of University College London on 'The Western World-View and the Inevitability of the Ecological Crisis'. He begins his chapter on 'The Concept of Stewardship' with the following words:

> A society which includes amongst its earliest and most tenaciously held beliefs a concept of its right to dominion over nature is faced with a paradox: the fullest exploitation of nature involves its eventual destruction. The destruction of nature involves, too, the destruction of that society itself.[4]

And later in the same chapter:

> The essential paradox remains: dominion over nature is incompatible with long-term sustenance. Only if the subjugation of nature is not permitted to proceed all the way to complete domination can a system of secure management be perpetuated.[4]

Along with the American historian Lyn White[5], John Black lays the blame fairly and squarely at the door of the Judeo-Christian theological tradition and specifically the early chapters of the Book of Genesis. In 1970 there was also an important debate going on within the World Council of Churches about attitudes to nature, and I remember being in Geneva with John Black at one of these exchanges. He had been asked a difficult question: 'Why, in the final analysis, should we fight to preserve species from extinction?'[6]

Put on the spot, Black listed some possible answers: first, the aesthetic (that they are beautiful); second, the ethical (that they have a right to live) and third, the scientific (that they are sources of genetic material or confer ecological stability). Beyond all of these reasons that people give, Black argued that there seems to be an unarticulated faith that somehow a wide range of species is desirable and ought to be preserved. This provoked a tremendously turbulent debate – even back in 1970 – and the Australian biologist Charles Birch caught the mood with his statement to the effect that – 'We need an ecological ethic, an attitude to nature which goes beyond mere usefulness. Otherwise, conservation is a lost cause.'[6]

This of course takes us straight back to Aldo Leopold in 'A Sand County Almanac'[7] first published in 1949 where he wrote: 'The land-relation is still strictly economic, entailing privileges but not obligations'.

This observation that still appears to live on in the minds of many landowners and occupiers of land. But Leopold went on to argue that the extension of ethics to address this problem is 'an ecological necessity'. In pursuit of his land ethic he then writes:

> (while) the individual is a member of a community of inter-dependent parts . . . the land ethic simply enlarges the boundaries of the community to include soils, waters, plants and animals, or collectively, the land.[7]

Many will no doubt consider that we have moved a long way from those earlier debates. Even official documents now speak in glowing terms of the concept of sustainable development as the lynch-pin of rural policy throughout Britain. There was even a 1990 White Paper on Britain's Environmental Strategy with an opening chapter on 'Stewardship' as the foundation of policy![8]

But I feel obliged to ask in a book conference on the future of Scotland's environment whether attitudes have changed sufficiently to have any substantial and lasting effect on the detailed planning and implementation of national strategies to conserve nature – whether in Scotland, the UK as a whole or the ever-widening territory of the European Union? We all should consider very carefully our response to that question.

CONSERVATION PRINCIPLES AND ETHICS

There are people here who have given a large part of their working lives to the cause of environmental conservation in Scotland – one way and another. There have indeed been some remarkable achievements, particularly over the period from 1949 onwards, but lets not congratulate ourselves unduly, as it could so easily be a little premature.

Most of the practical tasks of conservation management are dynamic, year on year, and it is that relentless pressure alone which draws down so much of the effort available. It also has to be said that some of that effort is becoming increasingly costly and needs to be more fully justified, not simply in the language of economics, but also in terms of the moral and ethical values of the wider community. In other words, we need to revive the philosophical debate about the fundamental principles of land management and environmental conservation in Scotland. It is possible that even the Scottish Parliament will wish to join this debate at some point as it is essential to consider the principles before beginning to draft the legislation, rather than the other way round. On this I write with some experience and feeling after 25 years in The Scottish Office.

Over that time Scotland has been 'hoist on a petard' constructed almost entirely to meet the requirements of nature conservation in England and Wales and not the more extensive needs of changing patterns of land use in Scotland. I refer of course, to the vagaries of the Wildlife & Countryside Act of 1981 as it stands, subsequently amended by later legislation, on the Statute Book. There is no way in which this cumbersome piece of primary legislation could be even remotely conceived as a 'Scottish solution to a Scottish problem!'

On the contrary, it is a Scottish problem seeking a Scottish solution: a point for MSPs to take careful note of.

The 1981 Act allegedly rests on the so-called 'voluntary principle' and arguments in defence of this principle have been regularly rehearsed in Parliamentary debates and committees as some kind of substantive assessment of the structure of the Act. In fact, the 'voluntary principle' has been used to conceal from the general public – and apparently also from politicians of every persuasion – the inefficiencies and flaws on which the edifice rests. I am not going to repeat the arguments here – but I have written several papers in various journals to that effect – and these can be consulted if you wish to read the more detailed case.[9,10] Even at Second Reading in the Commons in 1981, the then Secretary of State for the Environment had to make this confession:

The Bill is a compromise. It acknowledges that there is a balance of argument. It sets out the position to which the Government now believes it is right to move. It will not be the last Bill. It does not in any way seek to create a Maginot Line. It seeks a balance between the often conflicting and deeply held views of people whose motivation and sincerity are not in question, although they line up on opposite sides of many arguments.[11]

Well said, Minister, but what are you actually saying: 'Is it perhaps that you do not really see the Bill working very well in practice? Or have I got it wrong? Should we go back to the drawing board? Or should we just wait and see what happens?'

When revisited in 1985, UK Department of the Environment Ministers and officials still felt confident of their interpretation of the Act:

'The provisions of Part II of the Act depend essentially on the voluntary approach to conservation. The alternative would be the imposition of permanent statutory controls on farming and forestry operations. Instead the Act allows for temporary restrictions in certain areas while management agreements are negotiated whereby owners and occupiers forego the benefit of improvements to their land in return for compensation.[12]

The Financial Guidelines under the 1981 Act then enter the negotiating arena and the outflow of cash in compensation begins in earnest. The consequence is that the scarce resources available to the Government-sponsored conservation agencies, such as Scottish Natural Heritage, gradually begin to ebb away from more focussed conservation initiatives. This cannot surely be tolerated for very much longer in Scotland. The Scottish Parliament should therefore seize the opportunity to remove this iniquitous practice, which achieves little in the name of conservation and seems to go on alienating public opinion through continuing press attention.

In my opinion, the voluntary approach – a misnomer if ever there was one – is not ethical as it is presently conceived and translated in practice. As reflected in existing primary legislation, it represents a triumph of individual control and decision-making over the common good. It is no longer defensible, especially if we believe that attitudes toward the significance of the natural world have changed and are changing materially. In that sense, I believe that we are seeking to recover a much deeper sense of our moral responsibility for Nature and to apply a generally more constructive approach to environmental conservation in this new century.

This is a defining moment as we encourage the new Scottish Parliament to cast its eyes forward. The political leadership should not imagine that further prolonged and tedious amendment to the existing statutory framework for the designation of Sites of Special Scientific Interest will ever make a difference. In fact this could be the moment to recast the entire approach and create a further opportunity for the rest of Britain to reflect on the emergence of another distinctive period of Scottish Enlightenment.

In direct contrast to our own domestic experience, enshrining the 'precautionary principle' in the body of European environmental law does gives much greater cause for optimism and hope. This principle was introduced under the Treaty on European Union 1993, negotiated at Maastricht, and now provides the basis for all forms of environmental protection throughout the member states of the EU. The fundamental aspect of the principle is that 'in the absence of firm scientific evidence as to the effect of a particular substance or activity the protection of the environment should be the first concern.'[13] Further to that provision, the Treaty confirms that there is no need to wait for conclusive scientific proof before preventive action is taken.

In practical terms, the precautionary principle is much closer to the 'ecological ethic' which Charles Birch and others were strongly advocating back in 1970. The general acceptance of the principle therefore marks an important element of progress and could possibly act as the signpost towards a progressively more careful and systematic assessment of environmental risk as the natural precursor to any kind of development which could conceivably have a prejudicial effect on the quality of the environment, whether in urban or rural settings. Again, we need to think and act carefully to ensure that this becomes the working principle at the centre of all physical planning decisions the length and breadth of Scotland over the decades ahead. This should definitely be on our agenda – and we must be prepared to use the precautionary principle to maximum effect and positive result.

WIDER PERSPECTIVES

In 1992 the United Nations held the so-called Earth Summit (the UN Conference on Environment and Development) in Rio de Janeiro. Building on the platform first established at the Stockholm Conference in 1972, the Rio Declaration[14] asserts some key principles relating to the concept of sustainability – all of which have an ethical foundation, eg,

> *Principle 3*: The right to development must be fulfilled so as to equitably meet developmental and environmental needs of present and future generations.
> *Principle 4*: In order to achieve sustainable development, environmental protection shall constitute an integral part of the development process.
> *Principle 5*: All states and all people shall co-operate in the essential task of eradicating poverty as an indispensable requirement for sustainable development, in order to decrease the disparities in standards of living and better meet the needs of the majority of the people of the world.

Fine words indeed – but to a large extent, apart from the official UN statements, these principles also underpin Agenda 21[15] as the basis for future action at all levels of active concern for the environment, particularly at the local or community level. Agenda 21 is being translated in many important respects, albeit slowly, by local authorities, by voluntary organisations and by project groups through detailed environmental action programmes in many countries including Scotland. But progress has slowed recently as resource pressures have begun to take hold for various reasons. The meeting about the future for the environment in Scotland on which this book is based would therefore do well to endorse these principles and also the broad band of Agenda 21 initiatives. We should be attempting to carry them forward in our own work settings as effectively as we can. It is the kind of imperative which Governments are inclined to neglect, especially at mid-term.

On attitudes to nature and conservation principles, it follows that we all have an individual role and an increasing individual and collective responsibility.

Putting the economics and the resource problems to one side, we can at least begin to fine-tune our moral and ethical awareness when it comes to making decisions which affect the natural environment. Let us make sure that we attend to these duties and responsibilities in the interests of those who will come after us.

REFERENCES

1. D Bruce and A Bruce (eds), Engineering Genesis: The Ethics of Genetic Engineering in Non-Human Species, Earthscan Publications Ltd, London, 1998.
2. B Ward and R Dubos, Only One Earth: The Care and Maintenance of a Small Planet, Penguin Books, 1972.
3. P Stone, Did We Save the Earth at Stockholm?, Earth Island, London 1973.
4. J Black, *The Dominion of Man*: The Search for Ecological Responsibility, Edinburgh University Press, 1970.
5. L White, 'The historical roots of our ecologic crisis', in Science 155 (1967), 1203–1207.
6. D Gill, (ed), From Here to Where? – Technology, Faith and the Future of Man, World Council of Churches, Geneva, 1970.
7. A Leopold, A Sand County Almanac, Oxford University Press, 1949.
8. This Common Inheritance: Britain's Environmental Strategy, Cm 1200, HMSO, London, 1990.
9. J M Francis, 'Nature Conservation and the Voluntary Principle' in Environmental Values 3 (1994), 267–271.
10. J M Francis, 'The Uncertainties of Nature Conservation and Environmental Protection', in Futures Research Quarterly 13 (1997), 29–36.
11. House of Commons, Official Report – 27 April 1981, col 525.
12. House of Commons, Environment Committee – 1st Report Session 1984–85, vol 1, chapt 2, HMSO, London, 1985.
13. Treaty of Rome, Title XVI, Article 130r (section 2), as amended by Title II of the Treaty on European Union signed in Maastricht on 7 February 1992.
14. M Grubb et al, The 'Earth Summit' *Agreements: A Guide and Assessment*, Royal Institute of International Affairs and Earthscan Publications Ltd, London, 1993.
15. D Sitarz, (ed), *Agenda 21: The Earth Summit Strategy to Save Our Planet*, EarthPress, Boulder, Colorado, 1994.

Part Three. The Future

5

Key Issues and Objectives
For Sustainable Development

T Henton and R Crofts

INTRODUCTION

SUSTAINABLE DEVELOPMENT ARE two words which have begun to achieve a degree of currency within everyday language, at least within certain parts of the political scientific and business communities. They are used occasionally in news broadcasts and are the title of the Reith Lectures in spring 2000. The Earth summit at Rio in 1992 was when they first became widely heard and yet, despite the passing of nearly a decade, there are those who still maintain that, as they cannot find a satisfactory definition, they will not address the concept. This approach suggests that the discomfort of the subject is still causing some to remain in denial, rather than accept that business as usual for the world and its systems is not an option.

Sustainable development does not lend itself to pigeon holes of clear definition. It is, a journey, not a destination. It is more important to understand the issues and objectives for sustainable development and to look at mechanisms by which change can be effected, than to argue over the detail of a definition. This short paper aims to set out issues and objectives which the authors consider to be fundamental to the achievement of sustainable development.

BASIC PRINCIPLES

Whilst eschewing the need for detailed definition, it is nevertheless important to have a clear understanding of the basic principles. Sustainable development is a philosophy which demands an integrated view of the world. Over the last decade, in the early days of the concept, there was strong concentration on the environmental dimension, to the detriment of social and economic considerations. It could be argued that, in the last two years or so in the UK, the pendulum has swung too far the other way and that environmental issues are not being properly addressed as the social dimension captures the focus. In fact, sustainable development provides a framework for policy development and implementation which recognises the importance of the environmental systems which underpin life, economic activity and social development.

The philosophy recognises that the basic life support systems of the planet have limited carrying capacity. The croplands, grasslands, forests, oceans, freshwater and atmosphere all have a limited ability to absorb pollution and to be used effectively and, if any of these natural support systems is stressed beyond tolerance, then it will collapse. Dysfunctional environmental systems lead to economic and social devastation. If the systems are maintained and enhanced, they provide part of the natural capital of the planet. Renewable natural capital must be used sensibly, critical or non-renewable resources must not be used at a rate greater than that at which they can be substituted by other, preferably renewable, resources.

Much has been published about sustainable development over the last decade from a variety of sources including international bodies such as the UN, the EU and OECD through the UK government, its Round Table and the Panel on Sustainable Development as well as the NGOs.[1] The perspective from all of these bodies varies greatly and there is often a tendency, particularly with some of the NGO publications, to be exceedingly gloomy. In many ways, the gloom is justified because the enormity of the challenges faced by the world can be quite overwhelming and the lack of engagement, in even the earliest stages of debate and action, from governments, business and the public is depressing. Many politicians are refraining from positive contributions because they perceive the environmental movement as negative, stopping people from doing things, rather than appreciating the positive elements and the possibilities for changing peoples' lives for the better.

At the same time, society in the developed world is undergoing major changes in its relationships with governments and with science and technology. A fundamental mistrust has built up in the public mind which dismisses the contribution science and technology has made to the quality of people's lives. Leading thinkers in sustainable development[2] tend to have greater recognition of the fact that science and technology have a positive contribution to make to solving many of the earth's problems, even if some of them are its own legacies. A more sophisticated approach to the subject has moved on to recognising the need to aim for integration of economic prosperity, social equity and environmental protection. Society depends on the economy and the economy depends on the global ecosystem.

The subject is a complex one. It is a disturbing agenda for many people because it brings in ethics and values and starts to cross the boundaries of comfort zones. It is often easier for, say, the Board of a transitional company, to ignore the difficult issues of the value of natural systems, minority rights and fair trade than to embrace the new complexities of a rapidly changing world. Those who have chosen to ignore the thrust of the sustainable development debate have often come to grief in a short and spectacular fashion, witness the difficulties faced by Shell with Brent Spar or Monsanto with GM Crops. What the sustainable development framework does do is to allow issues to be properly linked and priorities identified. For example, fuel poverty, damp housing, poor health and excess energy consumption are all linked issues to which solutions can be devised through taking an integrated approach.

KEY ISSUES IN SUSTAINABLE DEVELOPMENT

There are many issues that could be classified as 'key' but six are considered to be of special importance. These are:

1. The threats and opportunities of globalisation,
2. How earth can accommodate its increasing population without exceeding its carrying capacity,
3. How fewer natural resources can be used still allowing social and economic progress,
4. How the preceding can take place with less waste and less environmental impact,
5. How changing patterns of consumption, demography and lifestyle can make development potentially more or less sustainable, and
6. How current real issues such as climate change, loss of biodiversity and environmental degradation can be dealt with.

Globalisation is without doubt one of the greatest challenges in sustainable development. The rate of change to the global economy has been exponential over the last decade and it is now a truism that 'nowhere is very far from anywhere'. This brings both threats and opportunities The threats lie in the increasing demand for goods, not just from the 20% or so of the global population which already claims over 80% of the world's resources and seeks more, but much more importantly from the 1 billion people who live at or below subsistence level, using less than 3% of the world's resources and who aspire to something above the abject poverty within which they exist.(3)

There are other threats from pollution, inequality, long distance transport of goods around continents, increasing energy use from fossil fuel and international agreements, such as the World Trade Organisation, if appropriate environmental safeguards cannot be incorporated. To balance these, there are also opportunities, often subtle in their development and presentation. These include common understanding of issues such as global justice, environmental shared responsibilities, accountability and the role of governments in the age of transitional corporations. Many of those corporations themselves are seeking to understand the new world within which they operate where the boundaries are often self set rather than by governments.

The continued population growth of the planet leads to heavy demand on its natural capital. Increased eco-efficiency is going to be essential if social and economic progress is to be made. There is a rule of thumb which suggests that for every 1 tonne of product, whatever that product is, 10 tonnes of material have gone into its production[4]. The rest is waste either in the form of emissions to atmosphere, liquid which is discharged to water, or solid waste which has to be disposed of somewhere. The inefficiencies of modern production will have to be addressed, with products being four or even ten times as efficiently produced, the Factor 4 or Factor 10 approach to resource use.[4]

There is a raft of issues around changing patterns of consumption, increasing consumerism, changing demographic patterns and lifestyles, especially in the developed world. Populations which are living to greater ages, combined with more single households, lead to greater demands on resources, such as water and energy. The increased mobility of people through personal transport is already recognised as a difficult environmental and political problem. However, these threats may be counterbalanced by the potential, but as yet unquantified, opportunities of e-commerce and 'dematerialisation'. The latter refers to the increased use of the Internet for all forms of business and pleasure which, it is postulated, will lead to a decrease in the need for physical presence of offices etc or to the need for some items which currently exist in material form.[2] The current changes and developments in the banking and insurance sector are seen as the first manifestation of this. This could open up many possibilities for more efficient use of natural resources and production of less waste but the potential social consequences are not at all clear. Finally, there are real and present problems such as climate change, the loss of biodiversity and increasing environmental degradation which have to be addressed.

OBJECTIVES FOR SUSTAINABLE DEVELOPMENT

An overall vision for sustainable development has to be the starting point for setting objectives and defining mechanisms for change. Such a vision should be founded on the following three principles:

1. People are part of, rather than separate from, the environment and therefore human society and the natural environment are interdependent.
2. The environment is one of the key capital assets of society globally, nationally and locally and for all generations.
3. The environment should be used for the benefit of people with the following provisos: actions are within the carrying capacity of the environment, the functioning of natural systems is not fundamentally damaged and that decisions about using environmental resources take full account of the risks involved.

If these issues are to be addressed there are several key objectives for sustainable development. These are:

1. To get leadership from governments and their Ministers,
2. To achieve integration into the mainstream of government thinking,
3. To manage globalisation,
4. To decouple economic growth from negative impacts on the environment,

5. To raise real incomes without irreversible environmental damage,

6. To engage people in all stages of decision making, and

7. To manage local Scottish issues to make a local difference.

All of these present real challenges for society. However, if progress is to be made then it must start at the top. Leadership from governments and their Ministers is essential if the concept of sustainable development is to be properly incorporated into all government policies. At present in the UK the government position is not clear. Sustainable development is discussed and acknowledged in policy documents and consultations but in reality it is not addressed where the most important levers of power are operated. The sector which seems to be making most progress is business where major UK plcs and international companies are addressing their 'right to operate' as part of their social responsibility agenda. Examples of this include companies as diverse as Shell, Scottish Power and Sainsburys.

The ambition to 'manage globalisation' is, of course, very challenging. It will have to encompass such issues as differentiating between global capital and global goods, how systems are developed to address this and ensure stability in economic and political terms, and the role of the knowledge economy. In conventional economics, growth is based on the use of natural resources. If progress is to be made towards a more sustainable economy, then the right signals must be sent. These will include basing economic growth on human resources rather than natural ones. Allied to the decoupling of economic growth from negative impacts on the environment is the objective of raising real incomes without causing irreversible environmental damage and the degradation of the earth support systems.

Finally, in a Scottish context, it is important to be able to realise the ambition set out in the Rio principles of engaging people in all stages of decision making. This is a common theme which has been propounded by the Rio Earth Summit by the EU, and by the UK and Scottish governments. It is a simple concept but one which in reality is difficult to attain. Some of the objective can be addressed by ensuring that all public bodies are presenting their data to as wide a public as is possible, using media such as the Internet, and ensuring that the data are comprehensible and well presented. The public understands complex issues much more clearly than it is often given credit for but it is incumbent upon public bodies to be clear in what they are presenting. Local issues need to be arranged in a local way which makes a difference. The adoption of Local Agenda 21 by many councils is a valuable way of facilitating this.

MECHANISMS FOR CHANGE

There are several mechanisms for change which are available and which could make a difference if adopted.

Education The fundamental skills of literacy and numeracy are essential in the modern world and will be needed by all citizens. Agenda 21 from Rio emphasises this, especially in the context of developing countries. However, in the developed world such as Scotland, there is no less a need to be able to work in the basic skills of the English language and numbers. Access to life-long learning is no less an issue of sustainable development than managing the environment. Education has a wider context as well. In order to change mind sets, it is essential that there are skill sets which can address scenario planning and the management of uncertainty, risk and change.

Information Provision of good quality information in a clear and easily accessible form was discussed earlier. Emphasis should be on reliability (statistical significance, error etc), comprehensiveness (covering all aspects of an issue and wide geographical coverage), serial (availability of time series and trends), and accessible (preferably through the Internet and Web sites).

Communication It is always difficult to decide how best to communicate with an audience but, whichever medium is chosen, it is essential to dejargonise text. Approaches such as 'decide – tell – defend' are no longer acceptable in the environmental context and skills such as stakeholder dialogue and talking with, not at, people are essential.

Structural changes Advisers on sustainable development need to be placed at the heart of government, in the UK and Scottish Cabinet Offices, not within individual government departments. It is only through access at this level that a difference will be made. Placing those responsible in Environment Departments all too often results in sustainable development being perceived as only an environmental issue for environmental interests.

Removal of administrative barriers These include ensuring that relevant planning guidance and building regulations are worded such that they encourage and reinforce 'good' practice and that all barriers to better environmental performance are removed.

Understanding the changes in society There are many subtle forces at work in society at present. These need to be harnessed in order that skills such as conciliation and consensus building can be allowed and encouraged to flourish. The advent of e-commerce and the Internet are all radical changes which can be used in order to achieve a more sustainable form of development.

SUSTAINABLE DEVELOPMENT IN PRACTICE

I. Sustainable Upland Management

A critical test of how sustainable development can be achieved in practice concerns the Scottish uplands. It is widely recognised that these areas have many functions for society: as a source of income for local communities and the owners and managers of land, as a source of recreational activity particularly for those living in urban areas, as a source of sporting endeavour for owners, visitors and paying guests, as a source of emotional refreshment for all groups in society, as a source of the majority of our water supplies to benefit all communities, as a source as some of our food, particularly lamb and venison, and as an area of international significance for its wildlife and landscape assets.

Economic circumstances in the Scottish uplands mean that in many areas agriculture and sporting estate management is unprofitable even despite substantial public sector support for the former and resource transfers by owners from other sources of income for the latter. Many consider that tourism seems to be the solution but there is intense competition in the global marketplace, resources from visitors can easily leak out of the local economy, and physical damage with consequent costs for restoration can occur. Wildlife and landscapes in upland areas are increasingly recognised as a major resource, albeit as a constraint by some because of designation to meet the government's international Convention and European Directive obligations. The uplands are also ecologically and often physically fragile. Sustainable development in these areas therefore demands a new accord.

During the second half of the twentieth century substantial change occurred in the land cover in the Scottish uplands. There was a loss of heather moorland and mires and a net gain of rough grassland and afforestation with commercial tree species. These changes were concentrated geographically especially in north east, east and southern Scotland. There are a number of reasons for these changes but the two most significant are high levels of grazing by sheep and deer and commercial forestry plantations with, ironically, both sheep and forestry being substantially supported from government funds.

A new vision for the Scottish uplands can only be achieved if the key drivers are manipulated to provide opportunities and result in beneficial effects. The table below sets out seven such drivers and what could be achieved with changes in policy and practice.

Table: Sustainable Uplands Management: Drivers, Opportunities and Possible Benefits

Drivers	Opportunities	Possible Benefits
Agriculture	Less intensive sheep grazing, encouragement for cattle, shift in income support measures to environmental management	Recovery of semi-natural habitats and wildlife, diversification of employment, opportunities for ecotourism
Forestry	Establish woodland/forest networks, agree principles of reasonable balance between forestry and other land uses	Biodiversity and amenity improvements
Sporting interests	Closer alignment of sporting and biodiversity targets (shift away from 'large bags'), better integration of grouse shooting, deer estate and salmon fishing enterprises	Improvement in standards of management, moorland restoration, reduction in illegal persecution of raptors,
Recreation and Tourism	Develop environmentally sustainable tourism industry	Promotion of responsible recreation improvements in wild land character, major improvements in paths network, more jobs
Renewable Energy	Cross-sector agreement on siting of developments based on integration of natural heritage with other interests	Improved siting of developments, creation of improved habitats for displaced interests
Extractive Industries	Strategic agreement on potential development locations	Greater priority given to wild/scenic areas, and to important geological/biological features
Conservation of the natural heritage	Manage areas for earth and biological resources, create networks of near-natural and biodiversity-rich areas	Areas managed for conservation may provide greater socio-economic benefits than some other enterprises

On agriculture, for instance, the European Union's Agenda 2000 provides a major opportunity for shift in agricultural support to farmers from production to a wider range of activities, including improved management of habitats and the species on which they depend and management of the landscape and recreation activities. Such changes would recognise the importance of hands-on management in the uplands through the labour inputs of experienced practitioners. As a result, we would expect to see the recovery of semi-natural habitats, which have been damaged or destroyed, providing a more diverse landscape with benefits to the range of wildlife in the area. As a consequence, we would expect greater opportunities for employment in managing the land in the uplands and opportunities for ecotourism.

Sporting interests have a significant role to play in the management of the Scottish uplands. Indeed, management objectives for heather moorlands, if properly implemented, can create ecological diversity and attractive landscapes as well as produce sporting benefits. However, a closer alignment between sporting interests and biodiversity and landscape diversity targets is required. There needs to be recognition that 'large bags' from grouse moors is perhaps no longer attainable as a result of the long term degradation of the productivity of these moors. Better integration of grouse shooting with deer management and with sheep grazing would also be beneficial. The outputs would, hopefully, be a widescale improvement in the standards of management through the reduction of grazing intensity, moorland restoration, and a reduction in illegal persecution of protected species such as raptors.

As far as recreation and tourism is concerned, there are few areas in the Scottish uplands where the level of visitor use is at or above the physical and ecological carrying capacity of the environment. There are opportunities therefore to develop a tourism industry based on the environment, provided that the environment itself is recognised as the critical asset of the industry. Promotion of responsible recreation by all visitors, management of visitor pressure by ranger services, development of ecotourism businesses and preferably the proper training and certification of guides are all possible and would bring economic advantages to these areas. At the same time, major improvements are required in accessibility, especially through improving existing and developing new path networks.

The sustainable development agenda demands that environmental, social and economic issues are looked at in an integrated manner. For the Scottish uplands there are a number of key objectives which should form the basis of sustainable uplands management.

From an environmental perspective, the distinctive elements of upland habitats and landscapes should be conserved. These are the most extensive near-natural areas in Britain containing highly valued species adapted to harsh living. The areas provide a sanctuary for society from urban-based lifestyles. Second, we should work within the capacity and resilience of the environmental resource. In doing so, we must recognise that the harsh climate and poor soils limit productivity, steep slopes and climatic extremes promote erosion potential, and there is a natural fragility of vegetation to external effects, such as air pollution.

From a social point of view, the first objective must be to achieve wider public good outcomes from the uplands. This should embrace the support to local communities in remote settings, putting in place means for achieving an improved demographic structure in the remoter upland areas and, at the same time, recognising the need of urban communities to use directly and benefit, indirectly, from the Scottish uplands. To achieve this, a new balance between national and local interests should be struck recognising that both host communities and urban communities have common and shared interests in sustaining the Scottish uplands and that financial support should serve to meet both of these sets of needs.

From an economic point of view, land uses should be of low impact and within the carrying capacity of the environment. This will mean a shift from traditional activities focused predominantly on grazing to a more diverse set of activities and with greater focus on and encouragement for managing the environmental resources of these areas. Overall, the balance of activity should not, individually or cumulatively, lead to environmental losses. There also needs to be recognition that the uplands deliver indirect benefits to the nation as a whole, for example, through clean water and organic-style meat. A greater recognition of the economic and financial benefits of these public goods should be an intrinsic part of future decision making about public support for the uplands.

There are a number of examples of how the environmental, social and economic components of sustainable uplands management are being brought together in different parts of Scotland. The Southern Uplands Initiative, for example, links development, amenity and wildlife interests through a series of local projects. The Moorland Working Group is a joint partnership between sporting, conservation and land management interests to develop novel techniques for resolving the conflicts between raptors and grouse moor management. Two major government initiatives and the supporting legislation are also relevant. The establishment of National Parks should bring about a greater integration of planning, development and natural heritage interests which will ensure the maintenance of environmental assets and bring benefits to host communities and wider society. The proposed legislation on responsible freedom of access to Scotland's countryside is based on a new contract between owners and managers of land and users with expected benefits to both sets of interests.

SUSTAINABLE DEVELOPMENT IN ACTION

II. Sustainable Urban Drainage

Scotland is a country which has high rainfall with many of its urban areas receiving between 650mm and 1000mm per annum. The problem of effective drainage which can remove both foul and surface water without causing pollution or flooding remains a challenge for every urban development today. Over the last 150 years drainage systems have evolved which direct both foul drainage and rainwater into sewers and from there into the nearest available watercourse. Investment in sewage treatment to protect rivers, lochs and coastal waters ensures that most of Scotland is protected from gross sewage pollution except where storm water overflows cause specific problems. The issue of surface water drainage originating from rainfall has provided a particular focus for sustainable development because of its diffuse nature, the environmental impacts and the fact that no one party has overall responsibilities for it.

The hydrological cycle allows rainwater to transport essential nutrients to plants and animals and is also responsible for shaping the natural environment through processes of erosion and sedimentation. These forces contribute to the landscape features familiar throughout Scotland. The hydrological cycle is one of the fundamental environmental process on which life depends, and needs to be recognised for its intrinsic value. In many urban areas streams are enclosed in underground culverts and residents are unaware that a watercourse is part of their environment. Modification of the hydrological cycle means that rainwater falling on urban surfaces such as concrete, tarmac and roofs is shed rapidly and effectively, rather than infiltrating into the ground. This modification has substantial environmental impacts. Where rainwater is drained via pipes to a watercourse, it cannot renew the soil moisture essential to plant life or groundwater supplies. During rainfall events water in urban areas is conveyed rapidly to rivers with little opportunity for attenuation of the peak flow. Flooding can occur readily in urban rivers with accelerated erosion and scour which damages urban river habitats. At other times, the reduced recharge of groundwater means that urban rivers are effectively running at drought levels for some periods of the year.

In addition to physical changes to the hydrology of urban watercourses, there are many potential sources of pollution such as litter, leaking oil from vehicles, sediment washed away from building sites or industrial areas, atmospheric fall-out from chimneys and animal faeces. These all give rise to a range of pollutants, not as the result of wanton negligence but reflecting the net-effect of human activity in the urban environment. The effects of these diffuse sources of pollution can be significant. When it rains, pollutants on the surface are washed into drains and flushed directly into watercourses, many of which are already stressed due to changed hydrological conditions. Pollutant concentrations build-up during dry weather and are mobilised rapidly when it starts to rain, therefore high concentrations of pollutants can enter watercourses when flow conditions are lowest. SEPA's monitoring shows that 20% by length of the poorest quality river water in Scotland is attributable to urban drainage sources.

It is increasingly recognised that the conventional approach of removing rainwater in urban areas is not sustainable. It is also clear, in the Scottish context, that no single authority can make all the changes necessary to bring about improvements. The first, and most critical, step in sustainable rainwater management in urban areas is a partnership approach to both the problem and the solutions. In Scotland, the Sustainable Urban Drainage Scottish Working Party (SUDSWP) has been formed to address the problem and to find solutions. Membership of SUDSWP includes the three Scottish Water Authorities, Scottish Executive, CoSLA represented by Society of Chief Officers of Transportation in Scotland (SCOTS) and

Scottish Society of Directors of Planning (SSDP), Scottish Housebuilders Association, Scottish Enterprise Lanarkshire and SEPA.

SUDSWP have developed the concept of Sustainable Urban Drainage (SUD) based on good practice in the USA, France, Sweden and Japan. SUD is a concept that puts the environment and people at the centre of decisions made about drainage. It includes consideration of both water quantity and water quality, along with the amenity value of water in the urban environment. SUD provides the opportunity to design a drainage system for rainwater that incorporates the need for flood and water quality protection, along with the chance to make a direct contribution to the urban environment through improvements to visual amenity by providing recreational areas and urban wildlife habitats. All of these considerations can be incorporated into a Sustainable Urban Drainage System (SUDS) for rainwater management in urban areas.

SUDS themselves can comprise one or more of the following structures:

- filter strips and swales
- filter drains and permeable surfaces
- infiltration devices
- basins and ponds.

SUDS are effective because they capture the rainwater at or near the place where it falls and attenuate the flow rate. This reduces erosion and the potential for flooding. SUDS also allow time for the natural processes of sedimentation, filtration and biodegradation, so that pollutants are captured and broken-down within the drainage system and are not transported to a river.

As there are a number of SUDS to choose from, drainage engineers, planners and landscape architects are able to select the best drainage option for the urban setting, taking into account a variety of factors that may be relevant at a particular site. This choice provides the opportunity to create an urban environment to suit local communities, whether it be the creation of urban recreational and wildlife areas around ponds or selecting a suitable permeable surface materials for a car park. Decisions made with the participation of the local communities are inherently more sustainable than those imposed from outside.

SUDSWP, in collaboration with CIRIA, have recently published "Sustainable Urban Drainage Systems Design Manual for Scotland and Northern Ireland".[5] This manual is an authoritative design guide that allows the principles of sustainable urban drainage to be put into practice for any new development. The manual highlights the need to think about drainage of rainwater from the initial design concept and for developers and the statutory authorities to work in partnership to develop drainage proposals.

Education is an important part of sustainable urban drainage, as people need to understand that SUDS are there to protect rivers from pollution and their homes from flooding. In addition, all the professional interests involved in development such as developers themselves and their consultant engineers and landscape architects, planners, roads engineers, the water authorities and regulators need to consider drainage issues at the beginning of the development process, in order to design the optimal drainage solution, without sterilising valuable development land. Education is critical to the successful implementation of sustainable urban drainage systems.

The concept of SUDS is not limited to theory. The largest scheme yet designed in Scotland has been incorporated into the Hyundai site and the associated housing, retail and road development to the east of Dunfermline. This scheme is a leading example of what can be achieved through close co-operation between all parties and is the largest of its kind built to date in the UK. Another similar scheme deals with "urban" drainage in a rural location at the Johnstonebridge motorway service station in Dumfries and Galloway. The large artificial pond there has attracted nesting wildfowl and is an aesthetically attractive amenity for the travelling public.

A sustainable approach to the drainage of rainwater in urban areas brings people and the environment into decisions that are made about land use and development. In addition, sustainable urban drainage goes some way to protect the natural hydrological cycle in the urban environment. A partnership approach to decision-making provides the arena for putting sustainable development in practice. Sustainable urban drainage systems allow for development to occur *and* urban areas to be enhanced to the benefit of Scotland's urban environments.

CONCLUSIONS

It is evident that the integration of social, economic and environmental issues will not be easy. Sustainable development challenges the conventional wisdom of how society is run and as such is uncomfortable for many people. There must be strong leadership from government, business and people who are in a position to make a difference.

In all the overwhelming evidence of environmental degradation and the other major problems such as the effects of climate change which are affecting the world, it is easy to overlook the fact that there are small changes which can make a difference. The literature has many examples of small improvements which, when added together, start to make a real difference.[6] Many of these achievements are hidden in corporate annual environmental reports which are published by companies or are unreported achievements of local action groups.

Finally, both SNH and SEPA are required by the terms of their founding legislation to take account of sustainable development in their actions. Both organisations try to ensure that their policies and actions reflect this important guiding principle. The two examples of sustainable uplands management and sustainable urban drainage are a manifestation of bringing together, in an integrated manner, the social, economic and environmental components of sustainable development into real life practical situations. SNH and SEPA seek to demonstrate how to achieve sustainable development in practice as well as to advise on the vision, policies and objectives and the leadership required from government.

REFERENCES

1. UN Conference on Environment and Development, 1992, Rio de Janeiro. 5th Action Programme on the Environment 1994, EC, Brussels. *Better Quality of Life: A Strategy for Sustainable Development in the UK*, Department of Environment and Transport in the Regions – DETR, London 1999.
2. P Hawken *The Ecology of Commerce*, Phoenix 1993. M Jacobs, *Politics of the Real World*, Earthscan Publications London, 1996. J Elkington, *Cannibals with Forks*, Capstone Publishing Ltd, 1999. A Giddens, *The Reith Lectures*, 1999, BBC, London.
3. J Vidal, 'Century of the Environment', *The Guardian*, 1 January 2000.
4. E Von Weitzacker, A B Loving and L H Loving, *Factor Four*, 1997, Earthscan Publications, London.

5. Industry Resources and Information Association, 'Sustainable Urban Drainage Systems Manual for Scotland and Northern Ireland', CIRIA 2000.
6. Department of Environment and Transport in the Regions, *Quality of Life Counts. Indicators for a Strategy for Sustainable Development for the United Kingdom: A Baseline Assessment,* DETR, London, 1999. Department of Environment and Transport in the Regions, *Sustainability Counts,* DETR, London, 1998. M Jacobs, *Environmental Modernisation,* Fabian Society Pamphlet, 2000.

6

Using Economic Instruments to Improve Environmental Management

N Hanley and D MacMillan

INTRODUCTION

Environmental problems are often attributed to the impersonal face of market forces. For instance, the expansion of private sector coniferous afforestation in the 1980s in sensitive areas such as the Flow Country was attributed to the availability of tax concessions and planting grants which made planting an attractive proposition. Similarly, the great expansion of agricultural activity in the 1970s and 80s and the environmental problems which followed from this are often attributed to the more favourable terms available to farmers once Britain joined the European Community. Economists would describe these types of incidents as *policy failures*, since they resulted from government intervention in the market which had undesirable environmental consequences. Economists also point out, however, that the market itself is often unkind to the environment, since environmental resources are not priced due to a lack of clearly defined property rights. The fact that firms face no market charge for polluting the atmosphere means they have little market-derived incentive to cut back on emissions. The fact that farmers receive no payment from the market for producing beautiful landscapes means that too few are produced in a pure market system. Both of these effects are referred to as *market failure*.

Governments have thus long intervened in the market on environmental grounds, seeking to produce a higher level of environmental quality than the market would produce. The environmental gains, be they in terms of lower river pollution, cleaner air or more habitat protection, are important from an economic point of view, since they constitute real economic benefits.[1] Thus, eventhough a cleaner river generates few benefits valued by the market, this environmental improvement has economic value if it impacts positively either on people's utility (a jargon term for satisfaction or happiness), or on the production activities of other firms (eg fishermen).

There are many ways in which governments can intervene to produce a greater level of environmental quality than the free market system would generate. Consider the example of pollution control. Regulation is one means of control open to a government agency, either in terms of insisting on reductions in polluting emissions, or in the adaptation of cleaner technology. Alternatively, the government can use persuasion, to encourage firms to adopt cleaner production methods, perhaps in order to achieve market-valued advantages from green credentials. Another approach would be to make use of the concept of legal liability, for instance through making firms liable for environmental damages associated with their actions. Finally, the government could make use of *economic instruments*. But what are these, and how do they work? We explain using the example of rural land management.

Economic instruments are policy interventions that change the financial incentives that land owners or managers face in such a way that behaviour changes to bring us closer to some social goal. By paying people or firms to produce environmental goods, more will get produced. Agri-environmental schemes operate in exactly this way, by offering a financial incentive for farmers to "produce" better wildlife habitats on their farms, for example, by restoring wetlands or extending farm woodlands. Equivalently, by increasing the cost of something, we can encourage people to use less of it. Taxing pesticides will encourage farmers to use less, or if highest tax rates are put on most environmentally-damaging substances, to switch to less damaging substances. Placing an environmental tax on nitrate fertilisers or livestock manure applications in catchments subject to eutrophication will encourage farmers to apply less of these potentially-polluting inputs to land. In a different context, putting an environmental tax on landfilling should encourage people to throw away less and recycle or re-use more.

Another approach to the use of economic instruments is the creation of tradeable entitlements in resources whose ownership was previously unclear or undefined. This also turns out to be equivalent to putting a price on such resources. For example, concerns are growing regarding abstraction of water from rivers, and associated environmental damages, during low-flow periods. In Scotland, abstraction rights are poorly defined. By creating legal rights and allowing them to be traded, we both control the total amount of abstraction allowed, and put a money value on the right to extract some specified quantity of water. Since water rights are now valuable, this creates a financial incentive for users (farmers or water companies) to use water more efficiently, since the decision to use more water for irrigation, for instance, means less rights are available to sell. Another example is the creation of tradable discharge rights to control point-source pollution, for example, from substances which exert a Biological Oxygen Demand. Again, two things happen: the total amount of discharge is controlled, and a financial value is attached to the right to discharge which results in a more efficient use of the assimilative capacity of a river or estuary.[2] A final example concerns the creation of tradable carbon credits in order to meet the UK government's commitment to the Kyoto protocol (see below). A key feature of all of these examples is that the government fixes the level of environmental damage, whilst at the same time making the right to use the environment in some way valuable.

WHY MIGHT ECONOMIC INSTRUMENTS BE A GOOD IDEA?

Just because economic instruments can help us achieve environmental objectives does not mean we should use them, since we have already seen that alternative mechanisms are available, namely regulation, legal liability and voluntary persuasion. For economic instruments to represent a desirable option, they have to be better in some respect(s) than these alternatives. Voluntary approaches which are not backed up with financial incentives or the threat of future regulatory actions are unlikely to be effective if avoiding environmental damages or creating environmental benefits is costly. We thus ignore such voluntary approaches from now on. Liability offers a realistic way forward in relatively few cases, so we disregard this too. The main comparison of interest is thus between economic incentives and regulation.

Economists have identified a number of important advantages for economic instruments, dating back to early work by Baumol and Oates.[3] These are as follows:

- economic instruments allow us to change the level of environmental damages or benefits in a way which permits more flexibility in response than alternatives such as regulation;

- an important corollary of this is that we can achieve an environmental target *more cheaply* with an economic instrument than with regulation.
- economic incentives produce a dynamic, on-going incentive for producers generally to adopt cleaner technology, compared to regulatory alternatives.
- in some cases, economic instruments implement the "polluter pays principle" (for environmental damages) or the "provider gets principle" (for environmental benefits).

The second point is the most important. By allowing flexibility, economic instruments allow us to achieve environmental objectives at a lower cost to society than regulatory alternatives. This can be proved mathematically for a wide range of cases where the cost of achieving environmental objectives varies across agents.[3] An alternative way of thinking about this is to say that, for a given total expenditure, economic instruments allow a greater level of environmental improvement than regulatory alternatives. Much empirical evidence now exists to support this finding in the context of industrial pollution control, both in terms of experimental work and from actual policy, for example with regard to the US Sulphur Trading Programme.[4] Evidence of the cost-effectiveness of economic instruments in the context of land use is also accumulating: see for example Shortle, Abler and Horan on non-point pollution from farming; and Hanley et al[5] on heather moorland conservation in Scotland.

We now look at four policy areas where economic incentives could be used to better achieve environmental objectives relating to rural land use in Scotland.

We now look at four policy areas, where economic incentives could be used to better achieve environmental objectives relating to rural land use. These are:

- Multi-purpose forests;
- Indigenous species: red deer and wild salmon;
- Managing congestion and erosion at outdoor recreation sites; and
- Agri-environmental policy.

MULTI-USE FORESTS

Forests generate many benefits for society other than just marketable products such as timber. These non-timber values include those associated with forestry's role as a habitat for wildlife, its value as a landscape feature, the role of forests as a location for informal recreation, and carbon sequestration values. These benefits have now been extensively studied in the UK, and economic estimates placed on them using techniques such as contingent valuation and the travel cost method. For example, Hanley[6] estimated the economic benefits of the Queen Elizabeth Forest Park for recreation and as a wildlife habitat. MacMillan[7] used estimates of recreation and carbon storage values for a range of forests across Scotland to re-calculate social rates of return. Hanley and Ruffell, and Hanley, Wright and Adamowicz[8] used contingent valuation, travel costs and choice experiments to estimate landscape values for a range of Forestry Commission sites; whilst MacMillan and Duff[9] report results on the non-market benefits of restoring native woodland at two sites in Glen Affric and Strathspey.

However, these non-timber benefits are un-priced by the market, so that forest owners get no reward for producing them. Whilst managers of public forests can and do take such benefits into account in their management decisions, this market failure has significant implications for private land-owners. The result is too few forests and the wrong kind of forests. One solution to this market failure is to make use of economic instruments. For example, differential rates of grant are now offered for the establishment/re-generation of native woodlands, relative to commercial conifer species. The high rate of grant available for native woodlands (£1050/ha), compared to only £700/ha for conifers, can be considered to be a greater incentive to produce forests with higher recreation and conservation benefits. The Woodland Grant Scheme is also spatially targeted, with higher rates of grant available for woodlands close to towns where there is considerably greater demand for recreation. There is however further potential to exploit spatial targeting in forestry policy. For example, Macmillan *et al*[10] have shown how the environmental benefits of native woodland restoration schemes could be enhanced by a carefully differentiated grant design using spatial characteristics. Carbon credits paid to forest owners by the market for the rights over carbon sequestered in these forests are also an example of an economic instrument which helps correct market failure. Such credits would be a major boost to the Scottish forestry industry and have been cautiously welcomed in a recent UK government statement:

> Because of the added complexities and uncertainties involved with forestry projects, the Government remains convinced that the UK's priority should be emission reduction rather than carbon sequestration. But the Government does recognise that forestry projects can provide environmental benefits and it is therefore considering whether such schemes should also be permitted within a domestic trading scheme. However, rigorous monitoring and verification of forestry projects would be crucial if they are to provide a credible source of tradable credits. The Government believes that the credits from forestry schemes should only be redeemable against carbon targets if, for example, the projects were consistent with forestry definitions and methodologies as set out under the Kyoto Protocol; the companies offering the schemes could demonstrate how the offsets had been achieved and could assess how much carbon had been saved and over what timescale; and a long-term management strategy was in place.[11]

Such caution is to be expected since awkward issues of the validation of credits, their lifespan and the net impacts on carbon lock-up (given that ploughing land releases carbon) remain to be resolved.

INDIGENOUS SPECIES: RED DEER AND SALMON

Red deer and salmon offer an interesting contrast, in that we seem to have too many of the former and insufficient of the latter. How can economic instruments be used to rectify these problems?

Red deer

It is widely acknowledged that the current population of red deer in Scotland is too high in terms of the balance between population demands and ecological carrying capacity. This imposes external costs on other land users, in terms of damages to forest stocks and other crops; and in terms of ecological damage from over-grazing.[12] However, the facts that estate values are linked to the number of shootable stags present and that the costs of culling hinds exceed the revenue so gained, mean estates keep stocks at too high a level. For example, in 1995–96, the hind cull was 2000 animals, less than the 27000 needed to prevent the population from rising.[13]

The emergence of deer management groups may be seen as one privately-led initiative to internalise some of the external costs of red deer, and produce more co-operative outcomes.[12,14] However, it is unlikely that these will successfully address the problem of ecological over-grazing, since the costs fall only partly on estate owners. How could economic instruments help? Three possibilities may be identified:

1 *a subsidy scheme for culling.* Regional and even local variations according to the expected environmental gains from reduced grazing pressure could be included. These gains will vary spatially and can perhaps be approximated by indicators of forest re-generation potential.

2 *a tax-subsidy scheme.* This would aim to be self-financing. Each area would be set reference levels for deer population. Estates who brought deer numbers down below this reference level would receive a subsidy payment per deer counted below the level. Each estate with deer numbers in excess of this level would pay a "deer tax" per head of deer above the level.

3 *a tradable permit scheme.* This could be organised in terms of either tradable entitlements to keep deer; or in terms of tradable cull requirements. So long as the costs of culling vary across estates, then such a scheme could reduce deer numbers more efficiently than uniform population reduction requirements (for details, see [15]).

Wild Salmon

Salmon stocks in Scottish rivers have been declining, particularly on the West coast.[16] Economic mechanisms have already been used by rod fishery owners, by buying up netting rights up-stream, and not using these rights. This has increased the number of fish passing up-river to spawn. However, bankside erosion, fish-farming activities and pollution all act negatively on salmon populations.[17] Economic incentives could be used to improve bankside habitat management, for example by making use of agri-environmental scheme payments to farmers to create margins around fields which border on rivers. The environmental implications of fish-farming on wild salmon stocks could perhaps be addressed by an environmental tax being levied on fish farms with the proceeds being used to regenerate wild salmon populations.

REDUCING CONGESTION AND EROSION IN OUTDOOR RECREATION AREAS

Although less of a problem in Scotland than in say the Lake District, concentrations of recreational users can impose externalities in terms of environmental damage (eg erosion and disruption of sensitive wildlife sites) and in terms of dis-amenity effects on other users (crowding).[18] The prognosis is that this will get worse, since the demand for outdoor recreation is rising.

Let us consider, in particular, erosion and congestion problems at a popular mountain site. One way of addressing this problem with economic incentives is through pricing. There are two alternatives:

1 access fees, for example through car parking fees. Charging for access to mountain areas in other ways (for instance, in a similar manner to US National parks) would be deemed impractical and highly unpopular. Car parking fees are perhaps more practical in some locations and have a similar impact, but may still be viewed as unpopular and as unfair to poorer households.

2 through increasing the time cost of access. Time is a scarce resource for everyone, especially leisure time! By moving access points further away, or by banning certain means of transport to sites (eg banning cars along private estate roads, or banning mountain bikes on estate tracks), it is possible to increase the time price of accessing a site. In fact, the "long walk in policy" is becoming more widely used in Scotland, for example in the Cairngorms.

Of course, if we increase the time or money costs of accessing given sites, we should expect pressure to increase at other, substitute sites. Hanley et al[19] have modelled this process using a data set of rock-climbers in Scotland. Table One gives some illustrative results, and shows the effects of car parking and time price increases both in terms of utility per visit and the number of visits.

Another issue here is cross-activity externalities in a recreation context. For instance, noisy water skiers at Loch Lomond reduce the pleasure of those preferring quieter activities at the site, such as fishing or walking. Should we impose a "noise levy" on skiers? This levy could perhaps vary according to boat engine size and would serve as a dis-incentive to those who value a day's water ski-ing least to change to some quieter sport, or alternative location.

AGRI-ENVIRONMENTAL POLICY

As we have already noted, farmers generate both positive and negative environmental effects through their actions. Positive actions include management which conserves semi-natural habitats, such as heather moorland, haymeadows and heathland. Negative impacts are associated with management decisions which degrade or reduce such habitats, and with non-point source pollution from the use of fertilisers, manures and pesticides. Again, as mentioned already, the market provides an insufficient incentive from society's point of view for farmers to generate the "best" level of environmental impact.

Agri-environmental policy has become an increasingly important component of rural policy in the UK as in the rest of the EU, and recent government announcements suggest that this trend will continue. The basic model is for farmers to be offered payments in return for management agreements which promise actions designed to increase the production of environmental goods, such as the semi-natural habitats referred to above. Take-up is voluntary. Total spending on initiatives such as the Environmentally Sensitive Areas scheme, the Habitats scheme and the Countryside Premium scheme in the UK was £86 million in 1997, and is slated to rise to £1.6 billion over the next 5 years.[20]

The overall evidence suggests that this use of economic instruments to produce environmental benefits in this way has been highly efficient, in the sense that benefits outweigh costs by a very considerable amount. This also suggests that increasing expenditure on such schemes would be desirable.[20]. However, it is also apparent that there is scope for considerable improvements in how schemes are designed, since for example the use of fixed-rate payment schemes means some farmers get over-compensated for the costs of participating.

CONCLUSIONS

Market failure means that it is desirable for governments to intervene in the pattern of land use determined by the market. Economic instruments work by setting a price on the use of the environment, penalising those who produce environmental "bads" and rewarding agents for producing environmental "goods". There are many advantages of this approach relative to the alternatives, including flexibility in response, long-term adaptation and cost-efficiency. We have shown how economic instruments might work in four examples for Scotland.

However, it would be wrong to suggest that the wider use of economic instruments would be problem-free. Important questions include the extent to which economic instruments are consistent with concerns over fairness and with the implied allocation of property rights. Some economic instruments also exist mainly to raise revenues for the government, rather than to change behaviour. It seems likely that the best policy direction is one which incorporates a *mix* of economic instruments, regulation, liability and persuasion. Currently, however, we feel the mixture is too thin on the economic instruments side.

Table: Impacts of increasing time or money costs of access in three mountain areas.

Policy option/site	Reduction in seasonal visits per climber, dV	Aggregate dV	Aggregate welfare loss, £/season	Welfare loss per reduced visit, £
A: Ben Nevis: car parking fee of £5	1.3	16,152	161,525	10.00
B: Ben Nevis: time price increase of 2 hours/day	1.85	22,986	155,312	6.76
C: Glencoe, increase time price of 2 hours/day	3.42	42,493	298,200	7.02
D: Cairngorm: car paring fee of £5	2.47	30,689	248,500	8.09
E: Cairngorm: time price increase of 2 hours/ day	3.49	43,363	285,775	6.59

Source: Reference 20.
Note: dV is the reduction in seasonal visits per climber

REFERENCES

1. N D Hanley and C Spash, *Cost-Benefit Analysis and the Environment.* Edward Elgar Publishing, Cheltenham, 1993.
2. J Shortle, R Faichney, N Hanley and A Munro, 'Least cost pollution allocations for probabilistic water quality targets to protect salmon on the Forth Estuary'. S Sorrell and J Skea (eds), *Pollution for sale: emissions trading and joint implementation.* Edward Elgar Publishing, Cheltenham, pp 211–230, 1999.
3. W Baumol and W Oates, 'The use of standards and prices for the protection of the environment', *Swedish Journal of Economics,* LXXIII (1971), 42–54. W Baumol and W Oates, *The Theory of Environmental Policy.* Cambridge University Press, Cambridge 1975.
4. S Sorrell and J Skea (eds), *Pollution for sale: emissions trading and joint implementation.* Edward Elgar Publishing, Cheltenham, 1999.
5. N Hanley, H Kirkpatrick, D Oglethorpe and I Simpson, 'Paying for public goods from agriculture: an application of the Provider Gets Principle to moorland conservation in Shetland, in *Land Economics,* 1998, 102–113.
6. N D Hanley, 'Valuing rural recreation benefits: an empirical comparison of two approaches', Journal of Agricultural Economics, September 1998, 361–374.
7. D C MacMillan, "Commercial forests in Scotland: an economic appraisal of replanting", *Journal of Agricultural Economics,* 1993, 44(1), 51–66.
8. N D Hanley and R Ruffell, 'The Contingent Valuation of Forest Characteristics: Two Experiments', *Journal of Agricultural Economics,* May 1993, 218–229. N Hanley, R Wright and W Adamowicz, 'Using choice experiments to value the environment: design issues, current experience and future prospects'. *Environmental and Resource Economics,* 11 (3–4) (1998), 413–428.
9. D C Macmillan and E I Duff, 'The non-market benefits and costs of native woodland restoration', in *Forestry,* 71 (1998), 247–259.
10. D C Macmillan, D Harley, and R Morrison, 'Cost-effectiveness of woodland ecosystem restoration', in *Ecological Economics* 27 (1998), 313–324.
11. Department of Environment, Transport and the Regions, *Tackling climate change,* DETR, London 1999.
12. N Hanley and C Sumner, 'Bargaining over common property resources: applying the Coase Theorem to red deer in the Scottish Highlands', *Journal of Environmental Management,* 43 (1995), 87–95.
13. P Gordon-Duff-Pennington, 'The price may be deer', *Landowning in Scotland,* 245 (1997), 23.
14. C Bullock, 'Environmental and strategic uncertainty in common property management: the case of Scottish red deer', *Journal of Environmental Planning and Management,* 42 (1999), 235–252.
15. D MacMillan, 'An economic case for land reform', *Land Use Policy,* 17 (2000), 49–57.
16. J Watt, B Bartels and R Barnes, 'Declines of west highland salmon and sea trout', Lochaber and District Fisheries Trust, Lochailort, 1999.
17. *Wild Rivers: Phase 1 technical paper.* WWF Scotland, Aberfeldy, 1995.
19. A Wrightman, *Scotland's mountains: an agenda for Sustainable Development.* Perth: Scottish Countryside and Wildlife Link, 1996.

20. N Hanley, B Alvarez-Farizo and D Shaw, 'Rationing an open-access resource: mountaineering in Scotland', Mimeo, Institute of Ecology and Resource Management, University of Edinburgh, 2000.

21. N Hanley, M Whitby and I Simpson, 'Assessing the success of agri-environmental policy in the UK', *Land Use Policy*, 16(2) (1999), 67–80.

7

Land Reform, Planning and People: An Issue of Stewardship?

J Bryden and K Hart

INTRODUCTION

THIS PAPER IS about the changing relationship between people and society, about the shift from state regulation to community participation as the framework of local decision-making. We look at this question through the lens of land reform in Scotland; and we focus, in particular, on the issue of 'stewardship' – a concept which appears to have won wide acceptance by most sides in the land reform debate. This concept provides a key to the history of land-holding in Scotland: from the confused potential of the present, through 20th-century bureaucracy to the feudal state before that and even to the fabled democracy of clan society. 'Stewardship' is an omnibus expression which appeals to all sides of the relationship between the state, non-governmental organisations, landowners and local communities. Apparent agreement on the importance of 'stewardship' may mask real conflicts of interest between different groups. As such, it could even be counterproductive to achieving major reform, by obfuscating what ought to be clarified. On the other hand, if communities are to play a larger role in the care of the land in future, the idea of 'stewardship' may be a useful way of building alliances and partnership across the interests and classes involved.

Scotland has the most concentrated land ownership of any western society, with 57% of private land being owned by 0.01 percent of the population.[1] In the light of this, the purpose of land reform must be to achieve a more equal distribution of land ownership and of the economic and political power which is associated with it.

The paper starts with a brief description of the land reform process in Scotland since 1997, and the proposals which are on the table in 2000.

Since land reform is about changing the relationship between landowners, communities and the state, we outline the main forms of social organisation that have underlain these relationships in Scotland. These forms are then explored in relation to the concept of stewardship. Finally, we ask if the discussion of stewardship helps to clarify the debate over land reform in Scotland.

LAND REFORM

The Government's outline proposals for Land Reform in Scotland[2] were announced by the Secretary of State for Scotland on 5th January 1999. These followed an intensive period of investigation and consultation by the Land Reform Policy Group (LRPG). The remit of the LRPG followed the Government's manifesto commitment to "initiate a study into the system of land ownership and management in Scotland". It was to "undertake a comprehensive analysis to identify and assess proposals for land reform in rural Scotland, taking account of their cost, legislative and administrative implications, and likely impact on the social and economic development of rural communities and on natural heritage". The group sought to identify the key problems, issues, and opportunities for reform. This work was reflected in the first consultation paper - *Land Reform Policy Group: Identifying the Problems* issued in February 1998.[3] A second consultation paper – *Identifying the Solutions* – was issued in September 1998.[4] The fact that well over a thousand responses were received to the two consultation papers indicates a high level of interest in land reform in Scotland.*

The Government's proposals were aimed in large part at the new devolved Scottish Parliament which came into being later in the year. During the parliamentary campaign all the main political parties, with the exception of the Conservatives, announced their proposals for land reform, and this revealed substantial common ground. The new Scottish Executive published a *Land Reform White Paper* in July 1999.[5] The main proposals were for three bills: one on the abolition of feudal law; one on community

---

* Measuring the 'interest' in land reform by the number of respondents in relation to the population of each region in Scotland, we can also note that of the 338 responses to the first Consultation Paper, 38% came from the Highlands and Islands, which has 7% of Scotland's population – by far the highest rate of response of any region.

rights to register an interest in land and ultimately to acquire it in the event
of its being sold, involving information on land ownership and right of
public access to land; and one on national parks. The LRPG did also make
several proposals which concern different mechanisms through which the
public interest in land might be secured. These included planning
mechanisms, community involvement and consultation and codes of 'good
practice' which may be linked to grant-aid approvals (measures of the
'cross-compliance' type).

Land reform, in its many guises, implies a change in the balance of
power between individual property owners, communities and the state.
The recent debates and current proposals on this thorny topic take place
within a historical context. There are several historical layers feeding into
what is going on now, especially in the Highlands and Islands where
feudalism and its tribal antecedents were quite recent and are still living
features of contemporary society. Tracing regional history back from the
current period, it is possible to link state-promoted communitarian
development initiatives to four phases of history:

1. Scottish devolution in the context of European Union: a renewed
   emphasis on local community, combined with a relative withdrawal
   of the state on terms still to be decided.
2. The modern bureaucratic state, a 20th century experiment in
   impersonal rule which can perhaps best be characterised as 'state
   capitalism',[6] the management of markets and accumulation through
   the nation-state, in this case the United Kingdom.
3. The feudal precursor of the modern state evolving over several
   centuries as a synthesis of personal and impersonal rule, typified
   by institutions such as 'the Crown' and the decentralised authority of
   landowners.
4. The pre-state social forms of the Celtic periphery, clan society, about
   which little is known and much is imagined, especially since they
   represent a possible historical precedent for contemporary initiatives
   aimed at communitarian democracy.

What is at stake in the land reform debate, as in the wider issue of
decentralised development, is greater democracy, more power to the
people. But this has been confused by the application of rhetoric derived

from modern planning and romantic nationalism alike to a historical situation that is, even more than most of Britain, the product of an uneasy compromise between feudalism and bureaucracy. Greater democracy requires changes in the way that individuals relate to the collective associations of which they are a part, in the way that social hierarchies and inequalities of power function in practice. How do people get more say in matters affecting their separate and common interests? If they delegate these powers to representative bodies or individuals, how are the latter made accountable, so that their actions may be seen to be the legitimate expression of the public interest?

Each of the phases of history outlined above may be said to have organised relations between individual persons and collective institutions in different ways and each remains a source of precedent for negotiating a way towards a more democratic approach to land ownership now. Clans resisted formal rulers; feudal domination was carried out by lords linked to kingship; and bureaucracy rests on the impersonal rules of office. In the 20th century, when the authority of modern states was never seriously challenged, no-one looked to historical antecedents, feudal or tribal, for alternative models of how to govern society. But in the 19th century, when it was understood that society was on the move, comparative investigation of pre-modern alternatives was an intrinsic part of the search for new solutions to the problem of organising society in the machine age.*

Our premise is that society is on the move once again and that the Highlands and Islands of Scotland represent an important crucible of that social experimentation which people everywhere are turning to in the wake of a retreating state capitalism. The main body of the paper takes up these questions through the issue of "stewardship", the idea of care exercised on behalf of others by a person or body responsible for assets held individually or in common. This is particularly relevant to the land reform debate, since the various competing interests are all likely to justify their claims in terms of the notion of responsible care or stewardship. Thus landowners justify their position as care for the land and its people; state bureaucracy in its guise as the Crown presumes to exercise that role in the name of eminent domain and representative democracy; communitarian groups use their

---

* Two good examples in the present context are Sir Henry Sumner Maine, Professor of Constitutional Law at Oxford (1890), and Cosmo Innes, Professor of History at Edinburgh University (1860, 1861, 1872).

closeness to the inhabitants of an area to assert their priority over the other two; and indigenous activists may even invoke an ancient clan democracy as cultural precedent for decentralized control of the land.

The invocation of notions like stewardship and community to legitimise claims for decentralised development through instruments such as land reform is thus particularly confusing. We live in times where conflicts of interest are frequently masked through the use of rhetoric commanding widespread popular support. In the remainder of this paper, therefore, we will explore how the concept of stewardship may be related to the various historical layers present in contemporary Highland society; so that, finally, we may return to the prospects for land reform there in the light of this discussion.

STEWARDSHIP

Stewardship emerges as a central issue in the recent literature on land reform and in the responses to the consultation papers of the Government's Land Reform Policy Group. The concept appears to be shared by a wide variety of interests. Thus the proponents of land reform, Robin Callander and Andy Wightman have argued that the Crown's ultimate responsibility for the management of land under the current feudal system amounts to a responsibility for stewardship.[7] Callander explains it thus:

> The Crown, by virtue of the sovereign rights it holds in trust for the public, has a responsibility for the management of Scotland's territory and its natural wealth and resources. This responsibility can be equated with stewardship . . . (7,p.117).

Several respondents to the first LRPG consultation paper from amongst landowners and non-government organisations argued that (good) "stewardship is more important than ownership" . In a note prefacing Robin Callander's book, the Head of WWF in Scotland, Simon Pepper, explains that the WWF equates stewardship with 'sustainable management' of natural resources, and that:

> stewardship, embodying the principle of legitimate use for human benefit – but with a duty of responsibility to future generations and

to the wider community – is a concept of increasing relevance and value in Scotland as elsewhere . . . .[8]

On the face of it, stewardship is a concept on which landowners and conservationists agree – indeed Ramsay[9] argued that it represented common ground between these two groups, and the basis for an alliance between them.

According to the Oxford Dictionary, there are essentially four groups of meaning of the word 'Steward':–

- an official who controls the domestic affairs of a household . . . servant of a college who is charged with the duty of catering;
- the title of an official of a Royal household;
- one who manages the affairs of an estate on behalf of his employer. In Scotland 'a Magistrate appointed to administer the crown lands forming a Stewartry';*
- an administrator and dispenser of wealth, favours etc., especially one regarded as the servant of God or of the people.

According to the *American Heritage Dictionary*, the word is derived from *sti-weard* or hall-watcher. *Weard* is related to aware and wary in being watchful; it is a similar word to warder, warden, guard and even lord, referring to someone who manages another's property or the household affairs of a large concern. In this, it appears to identify the person who would be responsible for 'economy' in its original Greek sense, *oikonomia* or household management. In the case of both economy and stewardship, an original focus on domestic affairs appears to have been extended in modern times to more public responsibilities. But we should remember that the great house of ancient and medieval times was often the most inclusive level of society.

As O'Riordan pointed out[10], the notion of stewardship is thus a very old one, and pertains to the management of resources on behalf of another or others. Its roots are not merely 'feudal' but 'pre-feudal'. However, the kind of 'stewardship' implicit in the old clan system was presumably different

* Walter, Steward to King David I in the 12th Century was ancestor to all the Stewarts, including Sir James Steuart, founder of Scottish Political Economy in the 18th Century. Skinner (ed), 1966, Vol 1 xxi.

from that which derives from the feudal system, as Anglo-Saxon law gradually replaced the ancient Celtic law and custom.

Three points are relevant for our present argument. First, when the charters conferring feudal property rights on clan chiefs (or those otherwise favoured by monarchs) were granted from the 12th Century onwards (David King of Scots) they concerned only a small amount of arable land. This, as Cosmo Innes pointed out, "is a narrow strip on the river bank or beside the sea"[11] p155). The rest of the land – the majority – was still held in common, Callander[12](p103) makes the point that "Millions of acres of common land survived the first five centuries of feudal landownership in Scotland . . . (b) . . . by the end of the 19th Century, nearly all this common land had been added to the private estates of Scotland's land-owners. Innes makes a convincing case that as the extent of occupation and use of land expanded, sometimes centuries after the original charters were granted, "our lawyers lent themselves to appropriate the poor man's grazing to the neighbouring baron The poor had no lawyers"[12].* Second, the Highlands were the last to be feudalised. Again, we rely on Cosmo Innes: "A clan in the Highlands before the fifteenth century lives in patriarchal fashion. The clansmen looked to the chief as their leader and father, but what we should call the common people of the clan held their crofts and pastures from father to son, from generation to generation, by a right as indefeasible as the chief's The power of the chief, from its very nature, depended on the good will of the whole tribe – for who was to enforce a tyrannical order?"[12](p157).† While we do not sign up uncritically for this romanticised version of Victorian anthropology, it remains at least an important myth which is deployed today by various interests in the land reform debate, and highlights the feeling of disfranchisement of rural communities, and especially the *Gaeltacht* since the 18th century.

---

* We are reliably informed that there is only one case in Scotland where ancient community rights of 'comity' have been reasserted on untilled forestry and hill land – in the highland parish of Birse, Aberdeenshire, on land formerly owned by the Bishops of Old Aberdeen . The Bishops had recorded these rights for posterity. These rights are now managed by Birse Community Trust. Robin Callander (pers.comm, 1999).

† A fact reinforced by the Celtic system of succession known as tanistry which, according to Innes([13],p176), "depended upon descent from a common ancestor, but which selected the man come to years fit for war and council, instead of the infant son or grandson of the last chief, to manage the affairs of the tribe

The chiefs, of course, got the crown-charter after lawyers discovered that clan lands "could not be held or vindicated, or perhaps could not have money raised upon them.".[12] In this way the clanspeople

> became altogether dependent on the will of the laird, and fell a long way below the position which they had occupied before the lands were feudalised. That, I think, was the most flagrant injustice inflicted by lawyers carrying out to the letter the doctrines of feudalism, which they assumed were the same with the old patriarchal occupation" (12)(pp157–158).

The main point for present purposes is that under the patriarchal clan system, the chief was claimed to have a duty of care or stewardship for the clan as a whole, and that was legitimised not by the State or the Crown but by the clanspeople themselves, at least in theory. Although it is very unlikely that this system was in any sense egalitarian in practice, it is certainly a very powerful myth which is not entirely without foundation. But we may also be forgiven for making a third point. It is that this history lived on to a much greater extent in the Highlands than elsewhere in Scotland for three main reasons: first, because of the oral traditions of Gaelic culture; second the relative regency of feudalisation (and remember that it took a further three centuries or thereby for the changes in titles to have any real effect); and third because of the brutality of dispossession in the 18th and 19th centuries.* This cultural legacy feeds into contemporary debates on land reform in all kinds of ways that need to be accounted for. It must be part of any explanation for why the Highlands, today as for the last two centuries, have been at the forefront of the land reform movement.

The etymology suggests that 'stewardship' is about looking after something not for one's self, but for another or others. There is a strong connection with the management of lands and estates, especially those of the Crown or nobles, and in the Gaelic with the continuity of traditional law and custom through oral transmission. In Scotland too, because of the link between the Crown and the Community of the Realm, and thus to the position of the Crown as Paramount Superior in Scots Feudal law, there is

---

* The remarkable survival of the culture, despite sustained efforts to stamp out language, dress and music in the 18th and 19th Centuries is to be noted, even if they were to have lasting effects down to the present day.[14]

some inference that the Crown is 'looking after' the land and other natural resources on behalf of the people of Scotland (a point strongly argued by Callander.[7]*

In relation to land, stewardship involves the way land is looked after, for whose benefit, and with what legitimacy and authority the 'steward' acts on behalf of others. Landowners and their organisations often point to their role as 'stewards' of the land or countryside. More enlightened landowners argue that their role as 'stewards' extends beyond the land to the people dependent on it for their livelihood. In this context, some recognise that whilst in the past the great majority of people in a rural community were either employed by, or were tenants of, landowners, this is usually no longer the case. Often too, they refer to the need to leave the land in good heart for future generations. In this discourse, the landowner is presumed to know what is best when it comes to acting on behalf of others, and there is no discussion of how he or she legitimises that action. It is a paternalistic discourse, rather than a democratic one. If there is broad agreement in Scotland that stewardship of the land is about caring for the land (and the people linked to it) on behalf of others, then the critical issues are: who is to do the caring, on whose behalf, and with what authority or legitimacy. Although the concept of stewardship and what it actually entails in terms of practical management of land is clearly contested,† there are even more fundamental and politically significant disagreements around these issues. Such disagreements are also linked with some of the most difficult issues to be faced concerning the relationship of society to the individual.‡ It is about what common rules governing the actions of each individual we agree to among ourselves; in other words, about the relationship between public and private rights and obligations.

As we have seen, the shift from pre-state to feudal society and land tenure in Scotland apparently involved a change in the relationship

* Note also that Immanuel Kant also considered that 'sovereignty resides or originates in the people'.[15]
† In recent times, the fundamental disagreement over the concept revolves around humankind's relationship with nature and related anthropocentric and ecocentric positions.[16] Closer to home, McHenry's study shows clearly the nature of the different constructions of 'stewardship' by farmers and by conservation bodies in Scotland:[17]
‡ Compare the nine propositions in Kant's 'Idea for a Universal History with a Cosmopolitan Purpose'.[15]

between the community and the landowner or chief which effectively transferred legitimacy from the community to the Crown. The Crown in turn claimed its legitimacy came from God.* At the same time, property rights were transferred from the community to the landowner and the Crown.†

The power which accrued to landowners in the feudal period was contested by merchants and then by industrial manufacturing interests from the 18th century. These conflicts, and the expansion of empire, led to the increased power of the state, culminating in 20th-century state capitalism. Powers of local taxation and the administration of local 'justice' were removed from landowners and passed to the state. In this period, the state took unto itself enormous powers, and became highly centralised. Especially in the period after the Second World War, it took responsibility for the welfare of people and, effectively, over the welfare of the land. It did so through the extension of planning and other laws, as well as by direct action such as that concerning national parks, the growth of various environmental designations and subsidy schemes and taxation relief's in relation to land use. In other words, the state took responsibility for a large part of what might be called 'stewardship'. Bureaucracy, held to be impersonal, took the place of the personal relations which characterised former periods. And the state claimed its legitimacy from democratic principles.

By the 1970s this system was looking shaky indeed. Challenges to the legitimacy of the state came from the unions and new political movements and from intellectuals of the left (Habermas) and the right (Hayek). The planning system was in disarray; the notion that a remote and centralised bureaucracy could somehow 'know better' how things should develop in local areas was becoming untenable. These challenges were reinforced by tendencies of globalisation, the collapse of the Soviet Union after 1989 and in the last decade especially by developments in the use of information and communications technologies. Increasingly, the call was for devolution of

---

* We are not here entering the debates about the 'moral economy' of landownership, and the idea of land as an inheritance – a common heritage of mankind –
 which cannot be bought and sold. These arguments, and their link with the idea of
 'stewardship' are discussed by Mather.[18]

† The same kind of processes are occurring today, if we care to notice them, in
 Amazonia, in India, in Thailand and in other parts of the world.

powers, greater involvement of citizens and 'communities' in decisions affecting their future, for a more 'holistic' notion of development, and for integration of the plethora of largely unconnected policies, agencies and initiatives. In the most general, and fundamental, sense, the issue of the relationship between individuals and their communities, between society and the state was once again at the heart of politics.

LAND REFORM, PLANNING AND DEMOCRACY

The debates around land reform have reflected these general shifts in political thinking and practice. Land reform implies a change in the balance of public and private rights and obligations over land. In the debates on land reform in Scotland, several prominent commentators have called for the retention by the 'Crown' of a statutory obligation of stewardship to be imposed on all landowners. Their proposal is to retain the ultimate superiority of the Crown, through the Scottish Parliament, after reform of feudal law. Whether or not such a proposal were adopted (and it is not part of the Scottish Executive's proposals for feudal law reform), the question of how the public interest in land is to be secured in practice remains.

In essence, what we can observe in the debate over land reform is a major shift from centralised, statist notions of land control, at the extreme involving nationalisation (an issue no longer on the agenda of any political party today), to notions in which 'communities' have a much greater role to play, whether by acquiring land themselves or by involvement in the decisions of those who do own it. We can observe the same kinds of shift in relation to 'planning' : here the current idea is 'community planning' where people are said to participate in plans affecting their future through their 'communities'. These shifts in thinking and practice are not comfortable for many groups or interests. For landowners, there is opposition to the notion that they are naturally the best people to exercise stewardship. Equally, for planners and professionals, there is a challenge to what they feel is their expertise. For environmental movements and specialists too, perhaps especially for them, there is a challenge to their conviction that they know best what stewardship is, as well as to their remote bureaucratic organisations and sources of power. For local communities, whose power over the land and other resources in their area has been systematically removed over at least three centuries by landowners and then by the state, there are challenges to get people interested and involved and to devise ways of responding to their new or at least evolving role. In addition, there is a fundamental contradiction in seeking to hand communities power over planning without altering the fundamental rights of landowners to decide outcomes affecting communities.

All of this is to some extent hidden from view by the use of synthetic terms like 'stewardship' and 'community planning' which can mean all things to all parties involved. We have seen that these portmanteau expressions somehow express the complex history of changing relations between individuals, communities, and the state since mediaeval times. If this can be the source of a shared conceptual vocabulary allowing diverse interests to make common cause at the local level, is the price paid in obscuring the real social conflicts at stake too high?

The issue in land reform is the extension of democracy and democratic practice. How, in a period when the power of states is diminishing and communities are being told in many areas of economic and social life to take more control of their future, can real power over land and other resources be transferred to local communities? How the state, in its new role as facilitator rather than director of operations, assist such processes; and how in that case should community power be exercised? Any concrete proposals for land reform must be judged in the light of answers to these questions. If they are to have a chance of achieving what is expected of them, they must be surely grounded in a realistic analysis for which notions like stewardship are hardly adequate, for the same reason that they may be powerful symbols allowing cross-sectional coalitions to be mobilised.

The consultation process on Scottish land reform revealed varying support for measures affecting the balance of public and private interests in land, as well as for differing interpretations of the concept of stewardship. Some difficult questions remain. For example: Can we be sure whose interests are evoked by such terminology? How are local community interests to be balanced against the wider public interest? What, indeed, gives the 'community' its interest in the land, when it has no legal property rights and can hardly be said, as it could be of the ancient clans, to be exercised in defending its interests against predators? These are some of the questions which must be dealt with if the LRPG and Scottish Executive proposals are to be seen as an adequate set of mechanisms to ensure the responsibility for care of the land on behalf of the people at large. On balance, it does not seem that such mechanisms would be strengthened by the introduction of a general obligation of stewardship on landowners through the retention of ultimate superiority of the Crown.

CONCLUSION

Bryden[1] has argued that if democratic and participatory local structures are to be held accountable for future development of communities, then their ability to influence the use of the land and access to it would critically determine the success of their activities . . . "The notion of 'empowerment' can only be realised under conditions which are not generally present under our existing tenure system and concentrated land ownership" (p104). Land reform, if it is to mean anything in Scotland, must be judged by whether or not it leads to more democratic and widespread ownership. Thus the two key elements in the LRPG's vision statement were 'increased diversity in the way land is owned or used' and 'increased community involvement in the way land is owned or used'.[2] Abolition of feudal law will not achieve either of these, nor will the creation of national parks or the formalisation of access rights. Of the proposals on the table,[5] the main hope rests with proposals for community right to buy. However, these proposals are deeply flawed by the restrictive definitions of eligible community bodies currently mooted, and by the absence of measures which would encourage sales of large land-holdings and reduce land prices to realistic levels.[1] Policies which could make a more significant difference to the current inequalities of land ownership and associated power in Scotland – such as land taxation, and residence requirements – are so far absent from the agenda.

The issues facing Scotland today that we have highlighted here include the need for a more equal and widespread ownership of land as a condition of economic democracy, and that for devolution of power downwards to local communities. The key policy questions are how these can be achieved in practice. If notions like stewardship (and we have touched on others such as 'community planning') point to a more constructive relationship between the state, non-governmental organisation's, local communities and individuals, and a more equal and transparent division of power between them then they may be useful concepts. If on the other hand they are used to obfuscate the real issues, such that no one knows what kind of power is being exercised by whom, then they merely constitute rhetorical devices cloaking the real interests and conflicts involved in the processes of devolution and land reform. As such they hinder realistic analysis of the issues, even if they may on occasion help to bring people together.

REFERENCES

1. J Bryden, 'A North West Scotland Heritage Area? A rural development perspective', *Nature and Man. Proceedings of the Conference on the North West Scotland Heritage Area.* Sabhal Mor Ostaig, An Teangue, Isle of Skye, Invernessshire, Scotland, 1991. J Bryden, 'Land tenure and rural development in Scotland'. *The 1996 John McEwen lecture.* A K Bell Library, Perth, Scotland, 1996.

2. J Bryden, *Towards Sustainable Rural Communities.* University of Guelph, Canada, 1994, Land Reform Policy Group, *Recommendations for Action.* The Scottish Office, Edinburgh, 1999.

3. Land Reform Policy Group, *Identifying the Solutions.* The Scottish Office, Edinburgh, 1999.

4. Land Reform Policy Group, *Identifying the Problems.* The Scottish Office, Edinburgh, 1998.

5. Scottish Executive, *Land Reform Proposals for Legislation,* Scottish Executive, Edinburgh, 1999.

6. K Hart, *The Memory Bank: Money in an Unequal World.* Profile Books, London, 2000.

7. R Callander, *How Scotland is Owned.* Edinburgh, Canongate, 1998. A Wightman, *Who Owns Scotland.* Canongate, Edinburgh, 1999.

8. S Pepper, Sponsor's preface. In R Callander (1998).

9. P Ramsay, *Land-owners and conservation.* In F Goldsmith and A Warren (eds), *Conservation in Progress.* London, Wiley, 1973.

10. T O'Riordan, 'Attitudes, behaviour and environmental policy issues'. In Altman and Wohlwill (eds), *Human Behaviour and the Environment.* New York, Plenum Press, 1976.

11. C Innes, *Sketches of Early Scotch History and Social Progress,* Edmonston and Douglas, Edinburgh, 1861. C Innes, *Lectures on Scotch Legal Antiquities.* Edmonston and Douglas, Edinburgh 1872.

12. R Callander, *A Pattern of Landownership in Scotland.* Haughend Publications, Finzarn, Aberdeenshire, 1987.

13. C Innes, *Scotland in the Middle Ages.* Edmonston and Douglas, Edinburgh, 1860.

14 J Hunter, *The Making of the Crofting Community.* John Donald, Edinburgh, 1976. J Hunter, *Last of the free: a millennial history of the Highlands and Islands of Scotland.* Edinburgh, Mainstream, 1999.

15. I Kant, *Political Writings.* Ed: Reiss, H. Cambridge University Press (1724–1824: tr. abr. 1970).

16. R Elliot and A Gare, *Environmental Philosophy.* Open University Press 1983.

17. H L McHenry, Understanding the Farmer's View: Perceptions of Changing Agriculture and the move to Agri-Environmental Policies in Southern Scotland. A thesis presented for the degree of PhD at the University of Aberdeen, 1994.

18. A Mather, 'The moral economy and political ecology of land ownership'. Paper for the conference on Land Reform and the Scottish Parliament. The Arkleton Centre for Rural Development Research and the Research Institute for Irish-Scottish Studies, University of Aberdeen, 1999.
19. J Locke, *Two Treatises on Government*, 1690.
20. H Sumner Maine, *The Early History of Institutions.* John Murray, London, 1890.
21. H Sumner Maine, *Ancient Law its connection with the early history of society.* Routledge, London, 1901.
22. A Skinner (ed), *Sir James Steuart: An Inquiry into the Principles of Political Oeconomy.* 2 Vols. Oliver & Boyd, Edinburgh, 1966.

Part Four. Overview

8

Scotland's Environment: What Future? Views from a Schools Discussion Forum

THIS EVENT WAS organised to complement the main Conference because it was felt essential to secure views of the younger generation on a subject of such importance to their future. Accordingly, students in S4 to S6 formed a Schools Discussion Forum. The topic was landscape and tourism. Students focused on how the benefits of a growing tourism industry can be balanced with the need to protect landscapes and the natural environment. Participants had the opportunity to learn from, and question the speakers, all of whom are actively involved in shaping the future of Scotland's environment:

- The role and importance of Scotland's environment – past, present and future (Professor Kevin Edwards)
- Tourism and the Environment: collision course or opportunity – the sustainability fix (Professor Roger Crofts)
- The role of economics (Dr Lucy O'Carroll)
- The role of public opinion (Professor Jeff Maxwell).

In workshop groups students then had the opportunity to discuss further and respond to specific questions and the following provides a summary of the students' ideas.

HOW DO WE MAKE THE CONCEPT OF SUSTAINING THE ENVIRONMENT MEANINGFUL TO TEENAGERS?

The conclusions, presented by Aamer Jabbar, were as follow:

- Education in environmental subjects is very important and should be a compulsory part of the school curriculum.

- Practical hands-on experience of the countryside through, for example, field trips is very important.
- Students should be thought to have respect for the environment, and to have thought for the future effects of present actions by society.
- More power should be granted to teenagers' opinions.

ON PREDICTED GROWTH RATES, DO YOU CONSIDER THAT TOURISM IS LIKELY TO BE BENEFICIAL TO SCOTLAND´S ENVIRONMENT?

The conclusion, presented by Sarah Speck and Ina Jahn, were as follows:

- Yes, provided that tourism is strictly regulated then there should not be conflict between the environment and the economic benefits of tourism.
- Both the environmental and the economic should interests should be made to work together to produce the best outcome.
- The importance of maintaining culture and landscape diversity should be promoted to the older generations.
- Tourism is good because it provides employment.
- Tourism cannot be relied on as it is a seasonable industry, however, this does give an opportunity for the environment to repair and recover.
- The environment should be seen as an economic asset.
- Tourism will be damaging to the environment, but the benefits should outweigh the problems.
- Guidance is the answer, not regulation. The new countryside code should be for guidance not regulation.
- Problems associated with tourism include litter.

WHAT CRITERIA SHOULD BE USED TO DETERMINE HOW LAND IS USED IN THE FUTURE?

The conclusions, presented by Imran Parvaiz, were as follows:

- Sustainable profit: grow what is in most demand, eg dairy cows, cash crops.

- Environment: look at the impact of fertilisers and pesticides and the benefits of crop rotation.
- Location: ensure suitable crops for soil types and effects on tourists' views.
- Public opinion: use questionnaires and feedback links on web sites to get people's opinions.
- EU policies are important and must be adhered to.
- Diversification: might have different crops suitable in different years in different fields.

WHAT EFFECT WILL PUBLIC OPINION HAVE ON FUTURE LAND USE?

The conclusions, presented by Katie Dalrymple-Hamilton, were as follows:

- Very broad. First Green Party MSP has been elected, representing a change in public opinion to being more environmentally aware.
- Demand has a large effect on what farmers grow, ie consumer power ('No' to GMOs and 'Yes' to organic foods).
- The public wants farmers to diversify (eg tourism) to reduce their reliance on subsidies.
- The public should have the opportunity to be educated about environmental issues so that they can have a better understanding and make informed decisions.

YOU ARE IN CHARGE OF THE SCOTTISH EXECUTIVE'S DECISION ON WHETHER TO BUILD A FUNICULAR RAILWAY TO GIVE SKIERS BETTER ACCESS TO THE SLOPES IN AN AREA OF THE HIGHLANDS RECOGNISED FOR ITS RARE PLANTS AND BIRDS. WHAT FACTORS WOULD INFLUENCE YOUR DECISION AND HOW WOULD YOU GO ABOUT MAKING IT?

The conclusions, presented by Colleen Osbourne, Sarah Wadeson, Jenna McGeever and Stephanie Gordon, were as follows:

Positive influences:
- Money generated by tourism allows for research and development for starting new businesses.

- New businesses will be attracted and new jobs created.
- Improved infrastructure for tourists also benefits locals.
- More recreational activities encourage Scots to holiday in Scotland.

Negative influences:

- Environmental damage by visitors to flora, fauna and landscape.
- Looks bad and is ecologically unsound.
- May not be economically viable.
- Funding: who pays?
- Tourists bring bad habits such as litter dropping and leaving open gates.

How to Decide?

- use questionnaires to ask local people.
- ask taxpayers as funders and users of the railway.

WHAT ARE THE BEST WAYS FOR GOVERNMENTS TO HELP
FARMERS LOOK AFTER THE COUNTRYSIDE? DO YOU THINK
SUCH GOVERNMENT AID SHOULD BE GIVEN?

The conclusions, presented by Colleen Osbourne, Sarah Wadeson, Jenna McGeever and Stephanie Gordon, were as follows:

- Government has a commitment to all industry in the UK.
- Farmers get funds from EU and this aid is vital.
- Today's farmers are businessmen and also countryside stewards. Aid encourages stewardship.
- Aid is a disadvantage when farmers get too dependent and it supports a sinking industry.
- So there are arguments both for and against aid. More studies would be beneficial to help decide whether to continue, increase or decrease aid.

TO WHAT EXTENT DOES A HISTORICAL PERSPECTIVE AID AN UNDERSTANDING OF PRESENT AND FUTURE ASPECTS OF ENVIRONMENT CHANGE?

The conclusions, presented by Brendan Hall, were as follows:

- Can make informed decisions if you have knowledge of past actions and consequences.
- Can look at how the climate affected the environment in the past and so help us deal with present climate change.
- Even if the analysis is not 100% accurate, some knowledge is better than no knowledge.
- See how the present situation arose.

ARE CONCERNS ABOUT THE STEWARDSHIP OF RESEARCH-BASED RAW MATERIALS (EG PEAT AND LOCH DEPOSITS, ARCHAEOLOGICAL MONUMENTS) JUSTIFIED AS FAR AS THE FUTURE OF THE SCOTTISH ENVIRONMENT IS CONCERNED?

The conclusions, presented by Patrick Lewtas, were as follows:

- Need wildlife and archaeological sites to gain information on past for the reasons above.
- New technologies in the future might allow us to gain further knowledge from previously studied sites, so they should be protected.
- Need increased awareness of the importance of such sites.
- Need better incentives and tighter regulations for landowners.
- Need incentives for landowners to report a possibly interesting site.

9

Summing Up

Sir Martin Holdgate

THE OBJECTIVE OF THE MEETING

THE NOTICE OF the Millennium Conference stated that the prime purpose was to try to define likely changes in the environment of Scotland and attempt to indicate the policies needed to enhance its quality and value to society.

I shall sum up proceeding under four headings:

- the constraints of environment and history;
- the social and economic drivers of change;
- objectives and instruments for sustainable change;
- the agenda for the future.

THE CONSTRAINTS OF ENVIRONMENT AND HISTORY

It is clear that Scotland has a diverse environment – a varied geology, steep climatic gradients, a great variety of soils, and a complex superimposition of human influence. From the opening presentation by Kevin Edwards and Chris Smout it is clear that, while Scotland has many ancient features, much of today's environmental character arises from massive and rapid recent change. To summarise:

- it was deglaciated only 10–15,000 years ago;
- it has experienced marked recent climatic oscillations, notably between the 14th and 19th centuries;
- its soils are young and began with high mineral status but have been progressively leached and acidified since then;
- much of the north and west is now peat-forming country;
- much of it was naturally forested, even in the Western and Northern

126

Isles, but forest cover fell to an amazingly small 4% by the end of the 18th century, only to rise to the current 19% by reforestation – mostly with non-native species – in the 20th century.

- agricultural settlement 6000 years ago boosted population, but since then large parts of the Highlands and Islands have been depopulated, while heavy herbivore pressure, especially by sheep, has been associated with biological impoverishment – creating what Frank Fraser Darling was to call an 'ecological semi-desert';
- industrialisation stimulated a further wave of rapid population growth but urbanisation and pollution have superimposed further stresses, and the country has become increasingly dominated by the town.

Scotland is what people have made it: and they have made it different things largely due to shifting politics, shifting economics and shifting social values.

Jeff Maxwell and Melvin Cannell looked to the future-speculatively because complexity implies uncertainty and there is a clear need for better modelling and forecasting tools. They indicated that the future of the countryside would be driven by a mixture of social demands, economic pressures and climate change. Sustainable development will demand a so-called 'accommodating' approach: sustainability will demand that we live within nature's limits and are able to adapt to changing circumstances.

The future of Scottish agriculture will be strongly influenced by European policies and world markets: outputs have been declining and Scottish produce may lose competitiveness against that of central and southern Europe. A more extensive use of land is likely, but in some places organic farming may expand, as may the production of distinctively Scottish goods for niche markets. The demand for recreation in the countryside will increase. In recent years, forests have expanded on to land coming out of intensive agriculture, with an increased emphasis on broad-leaved species (the natural dominants of most of Scotland outside the Central Highlands) because of their higher value for conservation and recreation.

By 2060 Scotland may have mean summer temperatures 1.6C higher than today, and winter temperatures 1.8C higher with 10 to 15% more precipitation, almost all of it falling in autumn and winter. Sea level will be 17 to 23cm higher, and it will continue to rise over the following two centuries. Tropospheric ozone pollution will increase, acid sulphate deposition will diminish, and acid nitrate deposition will increase and be a major ecological factor.

Maxwell and Cannell were relatively optimistic about the impact of these changes. The productivity of Scottish agriculture and forestry is likely to increase, and the pollutants will have limited impact. Wild biodiversity will increase, due to immigration from the south, but there will be some losses among the alpine and subalpine species, such as snow bunting and dotterel.

In discussion, it was suggested that the overfishing of the seas may bring a demand for more farming of marine fishes. As action to stabilise atmospheric carbon dioxide gains momentum, forests and peat soils will be increasingly valued as carbon sinks. There may also be an increasing demand for land on which to grow short-rotation coppice and other energy crops. Scotland has a substantial proportion of the total UK potential resource of wind, wave and tidal current energy – though the remote, diffuse and intermittent nature of these sources will mean new networks linking them to the grid: there will he controversy over visual intrusion in wild countryside.

Conservation will remain important, but will be 'embedded' as a component of multi-purpose land use. The management of access for outdoor recreation will be a major issue. Public values will demand debate among a wide range of stakeholders, and there will be complex trade-offs. If public opinion turns against field sports it will be more difficult to maintain heather moorland and open upland. The issue is one of choice: people can have the Scottish environment they want, if they are prepared to pay for it. But to achieve their goals they need to know the options and drivers available and how to manage change.

THE SOCIAL AND ECONOMIC DRIVERS OF CHANGE

The drivers of change will be climatic, political, economic and social. Enough has been said about the first. Economic drivers have been of paramount importance in determining recent trends in agricultural land use. Jeremy Peat emphasised that the future will be greatly constrained by Scotland's location with the United Kingdom and the European Union. EU policies and directives have a major – some would say dominant – influence on agriculture, fisheries, pollution control and nature conservation. But wider international actions under global agreements like the UN Framework Convention on Climate Change, the Convention on Biological Diversity and the World Trade Organisation will also have a substantial impact. The latter remains out of step with the others in not accepting the precautionary principle.

The political goal is development that is economically, environmentally and socially sustainable. Interpreting 'sustainable development' in tangible form is difficult, demanding a definition of terms and processes involving efficiency, equity and externalities. The Scottish economy has substantial environmental foundations, in tourism and service industries as well as in the primary sector. The thrust now is towards competitiveness, hampered by Scotland's location on the perimeter of Europe. Devolution has brought changes in the Scottish economy, but the influence of the Treasury, Bank of England and the Chancellor of the Exchequer, none of them accountable to the devolved institutions, remains profound.

One challenge is to development indicators of sustainable development that can link environmental and economic goals. Another is to internalise environmental parameters in decision taking. 'Green accounting', reflecting environmental values more fully in economic policy, may contribute here. The conclusion is that we need to understand how the economic objectives for Scotland interlink with other policy objectives, with quantified trade-offs and a clear articulation of priorities.

Social drivers of change are dominated by the demand for higher standards of living and an enhanced opportunity to participate. Public values may impel change: they may also demand retention of the status quo. The Schools Forum emphasised that education about the environment was essential, and has a key role in helping the development of social values – though a diverse society is bound to have a diversity of values and priorities. This means a need for much wider opportunities for participation, within a consultative apparatus that is far more transparent. Patricia Henton commented that public perceptions, for example of risk, must not be dismissed as irrational simply because they diverge from those of 'experts'.

John Francis discussed a particular set of social values – those reflecting our attitudes to nature, including their expression in an environmental ethic. Such an ethic is implicit in the World Charter for Nature, adopted by the General Assembly of the United Nations in 1982, and was the first major proposal in the second World Conservation Strategy, entitled 'Caring for the Earth', published in 1991.

Francis urged a debate on the principles that should guide conservation in Scotland, criticising current legislation, and especially the 1981 Wildlife and Countryside Act: the discussion implied similar doubts about development control legislation. His presentation made a clear case for a deeper debate as a foundation for environmental policy in Scotland. Is it agreed that the precautionary principle should be a central maxim? That in any uncertain situation protection of the environment should come first? That the actions of today must not jeopardise future generations? That there must be equity between the groups that make up today's society and between present and future generations?

SOCIAL AND ECONOMIC INSTRUMENTS FOR DIRECTION OF CHANGE

If the drivers of change are to be harnessed, and change steered in the desired direction, instruments of various kinds will be needed. But instruments are useless without a guiding vision – preferably a consensus – about the way ahead. Patricia Henton and Roger Crofts addressed the objectives for Sustainable Development in Scotland. They suggested that it demanded an integrated approach, but must focus on maintaining and enhancing environmental systems. Science, technology, economic prosperity, social equity and environmental protection must be linked within the sustainable development framework.

How? Henton and Crofts suggested a series of objectives (I noted they were all policy objectives, not environmental ones), and six mechanisms for action – education, information, communication, structural change, the removal of administrative barriers and understanding and working with current change in society. The need is to sustain the essential components and functions of environmental systems, to work within their capacity and resilience, and to secure outcomes that meet social needs and values. SEPA, SNH and similar bodies should establish frameworks for this process.

Management of land and environmental resources is clearly central to the future of Scotland's countryside. John Bryden's contribution seemed to me to follow on from here, for he examined the role of land reform, planning and the question of stewardship – a word also used by John

Francis. In Scotland, there is a strong pressure for land reform that will change the balance between owners, users, the wider community and the state. How does this fit with the concept of stewardship, claimed by some to be a manifestation of responsible land management on behalf of others, using resources sustainable and passing them on unimpaired? What social values are now driving the demand for land reform? Is there evidence that the present system is failing to achieve sustainability? Or is the driver a demand for involvement of a wider range of stakeholders in the formulation of land management goals? Care will clearly be needed to ensure that the demand for more access to land for recreation does not lead to a new version of the tragedy of the commons, because it diminishes the incentive of those who own the land to conserve it.

Once the objectives have been set (and means provided for monitoring and adaptation as values change), then it is possible to deploy instruments. Nick Hanley reviewed the scope for economic instruments, as a way of improving environmental management. The first point was that government needs to intervene if and when the market will not otherwise deliver the desired solution. this can happen because the market does not value environmental goods sufficiently, or penalise externalisation of costs. There are examples in the field of pollution control of using economic instruments to redress such imbalances – and some may well work in the countryside.

Indeed, we have examples such as payments to support traditional agriculture in Environmentally Sensitive Areas, and to encourage farm woodlands, hedgerow restoration and the like. We also have taxes on landfill and pollution. Tradeable permits are being established for greenhouse gas emissions and water abstractions. The argument is that people pay more attention to things that have an economic price tag attached. Economic instruments are often more flexible than regulation and achieve environmental targets more cheaply and efficiently. It clearly makes sense to reward the provider of "goods" and penalise the provider of "bads".

Nick Hanley illustrated his thesis with a series of worked examples relating to multi-purpose forests, red deer, salmon, congestion and erosion in popular mountain areas, the agri-environment , energy conservation and waste disposal. it is clear that these instruments can work, and are indeed working in very diverse situations alongside regulation, which remains necessary if there are absolute standards that must be maintained for the sake of public health or other essential interests.

THE AGENDA FOR THE FUTURE

Drawing on all these contributions, and especially the points made in discussion, I suggest that the Agenda for the Future should have eight components.

1. Educate and inform. Environmental education – including practical experience of the environment – is crucial. It will help inform public debate, and strengthen community commitment to the policies and actions that emerge.
2. Study the environment. We are still ignorant of many ecological processes and need better tools for forecasting and management. Support research as a vital investment in improved understanding.
3. Accept some absolute values, among them that the conservation of landscapes and wildlife enrich the spirit as well as the pocket. Conserve the irreplaceable relics of the past, and recognise that Scotland has a particular responsibility to cherish those environmental systems better represented here than anywhere else in Europe – or indeed the world.
4. Stimulate public discussion of values, priorities and risks and enhance the opportunity for participation. Open a debate now on the values which should guide environmental policy in Scotland. Provide new frameworks for that debate, and derive clear policy goals from it.
5. Recognise the constraints of environment and history and go with the grain of nature and informed social choice. Be adaptable, recognise that different goals and actions fit different circumstances and that new insights and needs will alter policies.
6. Look very carefully at the apportionment of responsibility for the management of land, testing proposed land reforms against the basic criteria of sustainable use and transmission unimpaired to future generations.
7. Explore the role of economic instruments and deploy them sensitively as means of influencing the community at large and individual citizens and industries towards sustainable goals. But be practical and

recognise that regulation must often define and enforce standards that nobody must transgress.

8. Recognise that the future of Scotland is intimately linked to the future of the rest of the UK and of Europe, and indeed the wider world: while sustainable development begins at home and must be grounded in Scottish values, its achievement will demand understanding of wider linkages. Ensure that Scotland plays its full part in influencing UK and EU policies, directives and environmental laws.

10

An Agenda for Action

R Crofts and G Holmes

SCOTLAND'S ENVIRONMENT – A DIVERSE AND CHANGING ASSET

SCOTLAND'S ENVIRONMENT IS one of our greatest national assets and is internationally renowned. Its rich variety of landscapes, flora and fauna has ancient foundations but has been subject to rapid and major changes in recent centuries and decades. These changes result from the major driving forces of climate change and the impacts of human endeavour.

LESSONS OF HISTORICAL CHANGE

Our environment is the result of both natural processes and human activity. [Appendix 1]. Changes in rural areas are driven by the needs of urban populations for food, timber, energy, tourism and leisure pursuits. In an increasingly globalised economy and society, rural and urban environments can no longer be considered in isolation.

FUTURE CHALLENGES

Decisions about the environment need to be informed by the likely effects of climate change, itself influenced by human activities [Appendix 2].

Current socio-economic trends affecting rural areas suggest a decline in the value of agricultural output, reductions in the numbers of farm businesses and in the amount of land in agriculture, and changes in its intensity of use. In forestry, we are witnessing a move away from purely economic objectives to the development of multi-purpose forestry, including greater diversity of planting and increased integration with other land uses. Other demands on rural land are increasing rapidly, including

134

widespread demand for access and enjoyment from urban populations. Land management will also include new forms of resource use, such as energy generation from the renewable sources of wind, waves, tides and crops. Changing social values may lead to desires for more proactive conservation of natural and cultural assets. All of these changes will present immense challenges in the future.

A FUTURE BASED ON SUSTAINABLE DEVELOPMENT

Our environment is what people have made it within the envelope of constraints and opportunities presented by natural processes. Our policies for the future need to be based on sound assessment of natural processes and society's demands and the balancing of opportunities and constraints. In particular, we need to recognise the need for local strategic planning and resource allocation and the balancing of objectives within a sustainable development framework. The Scottish Executive and Scottish Parliament provides us with the opportunity to create Scottish solutions to manage change within this framework.

A NEW AGENDA FOR SCOTLAND'S ENVIRONMENT

The future for our environment rests firmly in the agenda for sustainable development. Market forces alone have a poor record in managing environmental quality and delivering social equity. Intervention in the free market needs to be firmly based on clearly defined societal and environmental objectives. Within this framework, economic priorities should be developed with a clear understanding and evaluation of indirect costs and benefits – the so called "externalities".

The Government's commitment to placing sustainable development at the heart of all policies is one step towards the creation of a new framework of integrated decision making. **However, strong leadership is needed from Government particularly to set a vision and clear objectives**.

The proposals from the conference call for:

- a new ethic of resource use;
- new approaches to policy integration;
- new policy instruments;

- new approaches to legislation;
- new approaches to defining and achieving a healthy economy; and
- new ways of involving people.

These are consistent with the Scottish Parliament's aims of consensus and partnership.

I. A NEW ETHIC AND UNDERSTANDING OF RESOURCE USE

There has been a major shift in attitudes towards the environment in the last 25 years but much remains to be done. Sustainable development is a radical philosophy that challenges conventional wisdom. However, there remains a gulf between widespread acceptance of the principles of sustainable development and their translation into practice. There is a continuing need for education for sustainable development at all levels and in all sectors of society to shape attitudes. New opportunities for communities and individuals to contribute to sustainable development through their own actions are called for.

We need to agree absolute values on which to base minimum standards of environmental stewardship in order to shape the policy framework of regulation and financial incentives. These values need to reflect the importance of services provided by environmental systems to society and the economy. These services include clean air, drinking water, and healthy food, as well as natural defences against coastal erosion and approaches to flood mitigation.

A common understanding is required of what is meant by environmental stewardship, setting out a broad picture of how we want to use and look after Scotland's environment.

2. NEW APPROACHES TO POLICY INTEGRATION

We must recognise that the future of Scotland is inextricably linked to the future of the rest of the UK, Europe, and the wider world. We should seek to influence policy formulation at all of these levels. Sustainable development policies are influenced by government actions at national and international levels. Scotland must remain sensitive to its national and international setting and seek early involvement in economic, social and environmental policies, especially at EU and UK levels.

Agreement on sustainable development objectives for Scotland and the achievement of the integration of environmental objectives into all sectors is essential. The Scottish Executive and Scottish Parliament has begun the debate on sustainable development issues and their relevance, for example, to the Scottish economy. We would like to see equity and environmental concerns more centrally placed in these discussions and the development of sustainable development objectives taken on board by Scottish Enterprise and other bodies with an economic development remit.

The sustainable development framework should promote diversity in the use and management of natural resources and be flexible in response to local needs.

We must recognise the constraints of environment and history so that we work with the grain of nature and informed social choice. Although we know a great deal, we are still ignorant of many ecological and wider environmental processes and need better tools for forecasting and management and better assessment of possible attitudes. There is a need for further investigation and for the results to be presented in an accessible and understandable way for all of those involved in decision making. This may require changes in higher education, for instance, in the way research is commissioned and in the training on communication.

3. NEW POLICY INSTRUMENTS

New policy instruments should comprise a balance of financial incentives and regulation, derived from clear objectives and a shared vision, to manage a changing environment. Policy instruments are useless without a guiding vision, preferably a consensus, about the way ahead. The objectives for Government intervention in the market need to be clearly stated and measured. Government needs to intervene if and when the market does not otherwise deliver the desired solution. This can happen because the market does not value environmental goods and services sufficiently, or penalises indirect costs. It clearly makes sense to reward the provider of 'environmental goods' and to penalise the provider of 'environmental bads'.

There are some good examples of using economic instruments to redress such imbalances. These include agri-environment payments, grants for woodland planting and maintenance, taxes on landfill and pollution, and tradable permits for greenhouse gas emissions and water abstraction [Appendix 3].

The key to rewarding environmental stewardship is to recognise that people pay attention to economic price tags. Economic instruments can be more flexible and can achieve environmental targets more cheaply and efficiently than regulation. However, regulation can and has worked, such as in improving water quality, and should continue. Economic instruments should be used to encourage environmental stewardship and to deter environmental damage.

The resulting framework of policy instruments needs to promote diversity and to accommodate local needs. Indicators are required to ensure that the instruments achieve the desired objectives.

4. A NEW APPROACH TO LEGISLATION

Legislation should conserve Scotland's cultural and natural heritage for society, including its use as a resource for studying past and predicting future of environmental change. From an environmental perspective legislation has two key functions. First, it ensures that the services provided by the environment to society remain intact, and, second, it delivers local social and economic benefits. In this context, the environmental services include the conservation of our natural and cultural heritage for a variety of reasons, including its use as a resource to understand past environmental change. Our legislative framework sits in a wider UK and EU context. Those who impose policy and legislation should be accountable to the Scottish Executive, including, it was argued, the Chancellor of the Exchequer in setting the budgetary framework and the Chairman of the Bank of England in determining interest rates.

Legislation should be used to underpin minimum standards of environmental stewardship and so ensure that the services provided by the environment to society remain intact. The precautionary principle has been enshrined in legislation at the EU level (Treaty of Maastricht, 1992) and, at the UK level, the Government has adopted the precautionary principle within the UK Strategy for Sustainable Development. However, there remain fundamental differences between interpretations of the precautionary principle at international levels. The WTO has maintained that genetically modified organisms should be introduced and used until there is scientific evidence of harm. We need a better informed debate on these issues. Our legislative framework also needs to be better aligned to our social objectives and to provide the basis for implementation of sustainable development and the precautionary principle.

5. A NEW APPROACH TO THE DEFINITION AND ACHIEVEMENT OF A HEALTHY ECONOMY

New ways to measure the value of services provided by the environment to the economy should be developed as an intrinsic part of economic assessments and linked to indicators of sustainable development. We live in an increasingly market driven economy, in which continuing competitiveness is the key to economic success. This does not mean that environmental and social equity considerations cannot be taken into account in determining priorities for economic programmes. However, Scotland will need to continue to compete internationally and to maintain influence at EU and UK levels of economic policy formulation. We need better policy integration of environmental and equity values at the macro economic level (UK and wider) to provide the framework in which micro economic (Scotland and more locally) drivers operate. We need to find new ways to measure these values as an intrinsic part of economic assessments and link these to indicators of sustainable development.

Decisions on development should reflect a long-term assessment of the environmental, social, and economic costs and benefits. Society may be prepared to accept lower rates of income growth in the short term if this is associated with less negative or more positive externalities in the medium-long term. In order to reach such a decision, it is essential to have objective information and open debate on the extent and nature of trade-offs; to be able to place values on things which lie outside the market place; to understand the importance of environmental systems in underpinning economy and society and in identifying carrying capacities and critical resource capital; to take into account environmental services and damages in accounting procedures; and to develop indicators to measure progress.

6. NEW WAYS OF INVOLVING PEOPLE

Stimulating debate on environmental values, priorities and risks, and establishing a new programme of education for sustainable development in Scotland are essential. There are many examples, large and small, of good practice for sustainable development, including *Dùthchas* in NW Scotland and the Borders Foundation for Rural Sustainability. These provide a sound basis for greater involvement. Programmes of education for sustainable development should build on this experience and provide people with information, understanding and skills to help them to take better informed decisions and to encourage actions consistent with a sustainable future.

Strengthening the opportunities and providing support for communities to put sustainable development policies into practice, recognising best practice, and celebrating achievements are essential ingredients. The aim should be to promote community's engagement to influence and guide changes such as Community Plans and Local Agenda 21 projects. Encouraging local audits for sustainable development, assessing the environmental effect of projects and establishing local indicators of change are among the possibilities. Small changes and actions can make a big difference when there is community support. To make progress the accountability and legitimacy of representative bodies must be ensured, and all groups, including young people, should be involved in decision making and action.

IMPLEMENTING THE AGENDA FOR ACTION

Politicians and advisers across all parties in the Scottish Parliament and Scottish Executive and in local authorities and other public bodies have a responsibility for the future of Scotland's environment. The agenda needs to be reset. The proposals and suggestions from participants in the seminar summarised here provide a new agenda. It is hoped that these are taken forward and acted on.

Appendix 1

Effects of Human Endeavour and Natural Processes on the Natural Heritage

Both human endeavour and natural processes change the natural heritage. In the two examples below, the balance of evidence is for human endeavour on the one hand, and climate change on the other.

People have shaped the environment, at least since Neolithic times. Excavations on the River Dee near Banchory have revealed a massive timber hall and land management practices dating from about 3,500 BC. The substantial timber hall would have required a large supply of oak, and clearance of woodland would have been required to provide land for cereals and pasture. Later, alder and hazel spread onto previously productive land, and the area once devoted to arable and adjacent pasture became dominated by heather, acid grassland and bracken. This, together with studies on lochs elsewhere, reveal that soil erosion associated with agricultural activities of early settlers, reduction in woodland and farming practices resulted in landscape degradation.

People have had to respond to changing natural processes. Between 1200 and 1850, there was a 2°C drop in temperature which had a major impact on people and land use. Cereal cultivation at high altitudes on the Lammermuirs became impossible and had to be moved down the hill. Incidence of famine was especially high between 1550–1650.

Appendix 2

Possible Impacts of Climate Change on the Natural Heritage

Scotland's environment in the future will be influenced by climate change, and here we summarise some likely effects.

2050	Likely changes	Effects on Natural Heritage
Climate	Scotland warms by 1.6ºC (summer) and 1.8ºC (winter)	**Forest & agriculture** likely to adapt well: new crop varieties, increased range of crops, changing agricultural systems, more productive forests.
	winter precipitation increases by 10%	
	climate of Aberdeen will resemble that of Anglesey now	**Natural flora and fauna.** Overall little change, but serious local impacts. Flora & fauna of southern Scotland enriched, but few lowland species unable to invade acid moorlands. Local impacts: loss of alpine and subalpine habitats; loss of late snow bed communities; loss of snow bunting, dotterel, ptarmigan. Loss of coastal mudflats and salt marsh, unless intervention. Changing fish populations. Increasing risk of outbreaks of pests, including those on heather moorland.
	climate of west coast will resemble that of west Ireland now	
	more frequent more intense storms: greater risk of flooding	
Pollution	**ozone** continues to be depleted	damage to crops and some trees, and natural flora
	nitrogen deposition (and nutrient enrichment) remains high (vehicle emissions and livestock agriculture)	linked to declining mosses and lichen. Possible nutrient enrichment of heather moorland
	acidification (sulphur, ammonia, nitrogen oxide deposition) deposition remains high	acidification remains an issue

142

Appendix 3

Economic Instruments

Changes in financial incentives lead to behavioural changes and may be used to bring us closer to social or environmental goals. Two examples are given.

INCREASING AGRI-ENVIRONMENT MEASURES AND RESOURCES

Farming generates both positive and negative environmental effects. Positive effects of management for habitats such as wetland, haymeadows, heathland, and creating beautiful landscapes should be rewarded.

There is scope for increasing overall funding of such measures, more flexibility to ensure that schemes are locally beneficial and rewards for participating are fair, and better targeted to reward a broader range of environmental benefits. Current take-up is voluntary and subscription far exceeds available funding.

REDUCING CONGESTION AND EROSION IN OUTDOOR RECREATION AREAS

It may be possible to overcome congestion and erosion by using pricing incentives. Possibilities include:

- Access fees, for example through car parking. These may work in some areas but may discriminate against some user groups.
- Increase the time cost of access. Erosion at a popular focal point may be reduced by creating 'a long walk in'. This idea is being applied at Cairngorm.
- Impose levies on target user groups, e.g. in relation to recreation use of water.
- Pricing incentives targeted on certain sites need to be applied mindful of the potential for increased demand on substitute sites.

Appendix 4

The Royal Society of Edinburgh

The Royal Society of Edinburgh is a wholly independent body with charitable status. Its 1200–strong Fellowship includes distinguished individuals drawn from Science, Arts, Letters, Technology, the Professions, Industry and Commerce and from all parts of Scotland and beyond. The Society's independence and the breadth of the Fellowship combine to provide an important neutral forum for informed consideration of topics concerning the well-being of Scotland.

The Society was established in 1793 under a Royal Charter, for the 'Advancement of Learning and Useful Knowledge'. Today, it undertakes a wide range of activities, including the organisation of meetings and symposia aimed at the specialists and the general public.

As Scotland's National Academy, the RSE is ideally placed to work with and for the people of Scotland – a nation whose intellectual potential we want to realise.

The RSE contributes to the prosperity of Scotland through its links between sectors and subjects, independent advice and wide ranging activities and ensures that these impact locally, nationally and internationally.

Appendix 5

Scottish Natural Heritage

Scottish Natural Heritage is a government body responsible to the Scottish Executive and Scottish Parliament.

OUR MISSION STATEMENT IS:

Working with Scotland's people to care for our natural heritage.

OUR AIM IS:

Scotland's natural heritage is a local, national and global asset. We promote its care and improvement, its responsible enjoyment, its greater understanding and appreciation and its sustainable use now and for future generations.

OUR OPERATING PRINCIPLES ARE:

We work in partnership, by co-operation, negotiation and consensus, where possible, with all relevant interests in Scotland: public, private and voluntary organisations and individuals.

We operate in a devolved manner, delegating decision-making to the local level within the organisation to encourage and assist SNH to be accessible, sensitive and responsive to local needs and circumstances.

We operate in an open and accountable manner in all our activities.

For further information on SNH, please visit our website: www.snh.org.uk.

Index